THE FIVE
ARCHETYPES

THE FIVE ARCHETYPES

DISCOVER YOUR TRUE NATURE AND TRANSFORM YOUR LIFE AND RELATIONSHIPS

CAREY DAVIDSON

TILLER PRESS

New York   London   Toronto   Sydney   New Delhi

TILLER PRESS

An Imprint of Simon & Schuster, Inc.
1230 Avenue of the Americas
New York, NY 10020

First Tiller Press trade paperback edition April 2020

TILLER PRESS and colophon are trademarks of Simon & Schuster, Inc.

For information about special discounts for bulk purchases, please contact Simon & Schuster Special Sales at 1-866-506-1949 or business@simonandschuster.com.

The Simon & Schuster Speakers Bureau can bring authors to your live event. For more information or to book an event, contact the Simon & Schuster Speakers Bureau at 1-866-248-3049 or visit our website at www.simonspeakers.com.

Interior design by Laura Levatino

Manufactured in the United States of America

3   5   7   9   10   8   6   4

Library of Congress Cataloging-in-Publication Data
Names: Davidson, Carey, author.
Title: The five archetypes : discover what the elements reveal about ourselves
and our relationships / Carey Davidson.
Description: New York : Tiller Press, [2020]
Identifiers: LCCN 2019049595 (print) | LCCN 2019049596 (ebook) |
ISBN 9781982141714 (paperback) | ISBN 9781982141721 (ebook)
Subjects: LCSH: Self-realization. | Self-actualization (Psychology) |
Five agents (Chinese philosophy)
Classification: LCC BF637.S4 D3695 2020 (print) | LCC BF637.S4 (ebook) |
DDC 181/.11—dc23
LC record available at https://lccn.loc.gov/2019049595
LC ebook record available at https://lccn.loc.gov/2019049596

ISBN 978-1-9821-4171-4
ISBN 978-1-9821-4172-1 (ebook)

To Dr. Stephen Cowan, who reminds me in words, deeds, and character that the way of the hero is unconditional love.

May you hear the pain in their "no,"
May you feel the need in their pain,
May you follow the love in their need.

—DR. STEPHEN COWAN, MD

CONTENTS

CONTENTS

FOREWORD

Albert Einstein once wrote, "When a light ray is spreading from a point, the energy is not distributed continuously over ever-increasing spaces, but consists of a finite number of energy quanta that are localized in points in space, move without dividing, and can be absorbed or generated only as a whole."

What is it about light that inspires us, enchants us, and gives us hope? A beautiful sunrise can change the rest of your day. A deep red sunset can stop you in your tracks. My first memory of meeting Carey Davidson is of light. A kind of pinkish yellow glow filled the room we were meeting in to plan a workshop for children. Like a single candle in a dark room, her enthusiasm was palpable, the way I think Einstein thought of light as not just waves but packets of energy.

In the tradition of Chinese medicine that I have made my life practice, this palpable light is what it means to encounter a Fire type's energy. I did not know then that Carey was in the midst of enormous changes in her personal life, changes that would open her up and eventually lead her to create a center for healing in New York City where practitioners of all disciplines would be welcomed to share the space. I did not know the facts then, but I could feel the power of her energy. This "felt knowing" is one of the deep intuitive powers that Fire people like Carey innately possess. It is this Fire power that drew her unconsciously to notice the fields of sunflowers (*tournesols* in French) in France and choose Tournesol Wellness as the name of her holistic health and education center. Many of us, especially doctors, are taught not to trust intuition. It took me many years to learn how to cultivate it as a guide in my own practice. For Carey, though, her heart's intuition has enabled her to be open to learning, and this is what has inspired the book you are now holding in your hands.

We, as sentient beings, exist only in relationship. This is a simple fact. No one or thing can exist out of context. And yet so much of what we're taught, particularly in medicine, takes things out of context, and this has become a source of great misunderstanding and suffering today. In my training as a doctor, I found that these relationships were often ignored for the sake of efficiency and convenience. Seeing my patients feeling increasingly isolated and alienated by the one-size-fits-all approach to medicine, I sought alternative perspectives, and it was in Chinese medicine that I found a system of thought called the Five Phase model, also known as the theory of the Five Elements, that promotes growth and cultivation of the very relationships that connect us to one another and make us feel whole again. What makes the Five Phase model so unique is that it does not divide what goes on inside your body from what happens outside, nor does it separate what's happening emotionally from what's happening physically. The same patterns of relationships are encountered at every level of our life. This is as radical an idea as Einstein's recognition that light is both wave and particle. This model has changed the way I understand health and has empowered thousands of families in my practice to grow and thrive.

The core wisdom in this book is based on countless sages of the past who observed the way the five archetypal powers that comprise the Five Phase model—Wood, Fire, Earth, Metal, and Water—interact with each other. Because Carey is such an expressive Fire person, her enthusiasm is contagious in the pages of this book. Reading it, you will feel the excitement of discovering how what she calls the Five Archetypes motivate people's lives. What makes this book so successful is how well she herself has balanced her Fire enthusiasm with deep self-reflection (Water) and precision and gratitude (Metal), which promote her driving vision of health and success (Wood) in all relationships (Earth). Because she walks the walk, Carey's distinctive way of shedding light on this subject creates a reliable road map for understanding how to cultivate healthy, wholesome relationships in your life. May light shine in your life and inspire you to grow.

Stephen Cowan, MD
Tidewinds, Massachusetts

THE FIVE
ARCHETYPES

INTRODUCTION

When you walk into an unfamiliar room, you instinctively notice certain details—what different people are wearing, the "energy" in the space, the décor and style. You fire off decisions about who you're going to chat with, which people feel unapproachable, where you're going to stand or sit, and how long you're going to stay. It may seem that the motivations behind your decisions in this room are arbitrary and dependent upon your mood, as well as endless other factors—what you ate for breakfast, how things are going at the office, the norms your parents modeled for you as a kid . . . you get what I'm saying.

However, I'm here to tell you there's something that runs much deeper than the seemingly erratic feelings of a particular moment and the chance happenings in a day. You're not randomly cast hither and thither along a spectrum of emotional urges guiding you toward whether to make eye contact with a stranger, cultivate a relationship, or perpetuate one that's on its last legs. In fact, nature has its own highly personalized system of predicting your behaviors—one that, if studied and utilized, can set you on a course toward personal success and balance.

I call this the Five Archetypes method, and by practicing this system, you can not only begin to live a more mindful and fulfilling everyday life

1

but also foster more harmonious relationships with your loved ones, with your colleagues, and with every endeavor you pursue.

THE FIVE PHASES (ELEMENTS) OF TRADITIONAL CHINESE MEDICINE

Before I delve into the myriad ways the Five Archetypes method can vastly improve your life, it's important to understand its origins. The Five Archetypes method predominantly derives from the Traditional Chinese Medicine (TCM) Five Phase model. This is also often referred to as the theory of the Five Elements—that is, Wood, Fire, Earth, Metal, and Water—and how they help explain the ways in which nature grows and evolves, including how we as humans, as well as our relationships with other humans, develop. This thousands-of-years-old wisdom remains as reliable, unchanged, and unwaveringly valid as the rising and setting of the sun and the ebb and flow of the tides.

The practice of caring for ourselves and our relationships from the TCM Five Elements perspective is deeply rooted in the fact that human expansion and growth—in the physical, emotional, and spiritual sense—unfolds according to an innate, predetermined natural code. This enduring code comprises all the laws of nature and applies as equally to the earth's elements, to the seasons, and to farming as it does to our human processes such as learning, healing, and the creation and dissolution of interpersonal relationships. This system of understanding the complex influences and building blocks of our environment and of the human mind, body, and spirit serves as the seat of much of Chinese medicine practice today.

The TCM theory of the Five Elements suggests that when we live a life aligned with our own true nature and compassionately empathize with the diverse gifts that others bring to the table, we experience a loving, forgiving, and predictable flow in our lives. Just as a beautiful sunflower responds with grace and predictability to the push and pull of the migrating sun across the sky, a person who understands the natural phases of the Five Elements of nature and human development lives a more gentle and sublime life. She is reconciled and at ease with her own strengths, challenges, motivations, and preoccupations. She thrives knowing and celebrating who she is instead of aching and fighting against her nature to become something misaligned with her very soul.

According to Chinese medicine, the elements exist in a specific order that correlates to other natural cycles, such as times of day and seasons of the year. For example, Wood corresponds to spring, Fire to summer, Earth to early fall (when many farmers typically harvest crops), Metal to autumn, and Water to winter.

From an interpersonal behavioral perspective, the Five Elements also interact with and influence one another in distinct fashion. Depending on the situation, certain elements can pleasantly encourage and nurture other elements, while others can be irritating challengers. The images below and on the following page illustrate this.

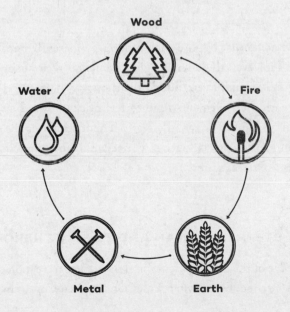

The elements that occur in the diagram directly before and directly after one another are instinctively soothing to each other. They replenish one another's energy and calm each other down in times of tension.

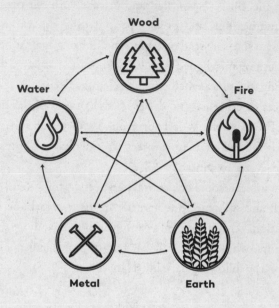

The elements that oppose each other are inherently bothersome to each other. However, these challenging elemental relationships are important to understand. Even though the thoughts, habits, and behaviors associated with these elements tend to feel prickly toward one another, this built-in discomfort is actually a gift. The irritation is the exact clue that helps us identify precisely what we need to do in order to balance out our overreactive stress states.

DR. STEPHEN COWAN AND THE FIVE HEROES

My knowledge of the Five Elements, and my eventual creation of the Five Archetypes method, began when I met Dr. Stephen Cowan in 2013. He and I were part of a small group of people working together to create a program to teach mindfulness to parents and children. Dr. Cowan was introduced to me as a world-renowned, board-certified integrative developmental pediatrician with more than thirty years of clinical experience working with children. He had developed a unique, holistic approach to evaluating and treating children struggling with chronic physical, emotional, and cognitive disorders. In fact, considering the child as a reflection of the interrelated forces of family and environment is the central focus of his practice. This approach respects the inseparability of mind, body, and spirit and promotes a deeper understanding of what it means to be healthy. Over the course of his career, Dr. Cowan has cared for thousands of children, has reached thousands of readers, and has taught hundreds of students. I recall from those early meetings with him that he exuded a gentle but palpable and robust power.

I can't say I remember much detail about the planning meetings for the mindfulness program other than that it was a bear trying to coordinate the schedules of the seven or eight of us in the group. However, I was intuitively drawn to stay in contact with Dr. Cowan after the program ended. Six months after running into him at the annual Integrative Healthcare Symposium in New York City, I emailed him to let him know I had opened Tournesol Wellness, an integrative health center. Not long after, Dr. Cowan moved his New York City office location to Tournesol, and I was fortunate to get to see him every week.

Witnessing the regular flow of parents visiting Dr. Cowan at Tournesol for answers to complex issues and then leaving with a proverbial weight lifted piqued my curiosity about the focus of his practice. I began to intensely study Dr. Cowan's methods through conversations with him and by reading his book, *Fire Child, Water Child: How Understanding the Five Types of ADHD Can Help You Improve Your Child's Self-Esteem and Attention*, which adapts the Five Elements theory of TCM to illustrate the different types of "heroes" kids with ADHD can be, with each hero type corresponding to one of the Five Elements. In a very short time, I realized that Dr. Cowan's work had led to the creation of a practical, reliable, compassionate, and brilliant system for parents who want to help their children grow into flourishing, high-functioning young adults. As a mom of three with more of a holistic-leaning philosophy on health, this system deeply resonated with me, and it ultimately inspired me to develop the Five Archetypes method that I use every day in my work with individuals and companies at Tournesol.

◆ ◆ ◆ ◆ ◆

My practice is chock-full of people who want answers and directions. They're seeking relief from what they perceive as a life of chaos. Motivated by a resounding need to ease physical discomfort, confusion, and uncomfortable emotions, they want a holistic and empowering way out of feeling crappy, and they want it *now*.

Before meeting Dr. Cowan and learning about his Five Heroes philosophy, as well as its TCM and Five Phase model origins, I was eager to find a way to better collate and utilize the myriad healthy lifestyle strategies I had learned over the years. With all the advanced technology and cogent minds that are devoted to developing wellness solutions, I wondered why so many people of all backgrounds still suffered dearly with difficult relationships and mental instability. I often wished there were something available to us that was universal, unchanging, and personalized, yet easy to learn and follow. I was seeking something that had a forever shelf life and could stand the test of time, along with having the agility to grow, expand, and evolve with us.

When Dr. Cowan introduced me to the TCM theory of the Five Elements, an awareness within me flickered. You see, I had personally been seeking the holistic panacea for almost five years. I wanted to find the magic pill to cure my own emotional unrest, and for some time I was positive that I would find it all wrapped up in green juice or intermittent fasting. But I hadn't found what I was seeking for all that time because I was looking for something that didn't exist. I was seeking the "how" instead of pursuing the "what."

Like many of us, I wanted to know "how" to make the discomfort stop so I could keep plowing forward with my to-do list. It didn't occur to me that my achiness was an indicator, an invitation to look further into "what" was at the root of my uncomfortable challenges. To make lasting life improvements, I needed to know what was going on inside me that led me to resist facing my challenges. But first I had to learn how to develop the skill of seeing myself from a more compassionate perspective.

I learned from Dr. Cowan that my "how" mind-set was incongruent with the empowered outcome I was seeking. We are beings in a constant state of flux. From the smallest vibration of our cellular behavior to the most astounding of life-affirming convictions, our endeavor to achieve bliss, harmony, and balance is perpetual. Our physical body seeks homeostasis in an environment where the proverbial goalpost is always moving. Why would I expect a different reality in my social and emotional life? I discovered that there really is no rest, nor any quick fix for the weary.

Another reason my search for a singular solution left me at a loss was that I couldn't expect to address a multifaceted challenge by targeting only one aspect of the problem. Stubborn challenges affect us on the physical, emotional, and spiritual levels. By merely addressing one of these components, we only partially suture the wound.

While exploring the idea of heroic growth with Dr. Cowan in my early days of knowing him, I concluded that my belief in a one-size-fits-all, unidimensional "cure" was flawed. The only way to achieve ongoing radiant strength was by personalizing my efforts and employing a multimodal approach, addressing all three interwoven body, mind, and spirit aspects of well-being—which led me to the next conundrum. The lack of an easy and quick fix wasn't going to be attractive to many of the people I wanted to help. The solution was to be found in doing more work—and unless a person was suffering a lot, more work usually equaled "No thank you." It seemed that the only complete and effective way for people to live a life of strength and resilience was to believe and do the following:

+ Give a darn. Care about doing this work for yourself, your loved ones, and the global community.
+ Show up every day and do the work. This isn't a one and done. Commit to practice, because this is about skill building and forming new habits. You wouldn't stop exercising your biceps once you liked how they looked, right?
+ Release your need to be right. Open up to the idea that you can learn from everyone and everything in your environment. We never stop growing.
+ Think with your heart, because logic can sometimes block your ability to be compassionate to yourself and others.

So how do I make that fresh perspective and mountain of effort attractive to my worried, always-on-the-run clientele at Tournesol? Unfortunately, there isn't an easy answer to that question. My optimism drives me to believe that we're on the cusp of a seismic shift in how we perceive and achieve emotional, physical, and spiritual success. But at this point, I still see a lot of people who wait until their aches and pains are chronic before looking for a way out of discomfort. It takes a lot of time out of a busy day to pause and evaluate one's needs for building, and sticking to, a personalized and proactive health plan. I think we're moving toward a culture in which pursuing prevention is the norm, but we haven't yet reached the tipping point.

There's certainly a rumbling and an undercurrent of people who don't like how they feel every day and want to know what they can do for themselves. They want to feel empowered and more in control of their destiny with knowledge and skills. I was part of that panacea-seeking squall, and

I'm a surefire member of the undercurrent. I wished for that road map. I wanted to know what to do to feel better all the time. I yearned to understand why I got stuck repeating patterns that kept me from progressing. I wanted to soar, to have a good life.

I found that the only answer that has made complete sense to me is the Five Archetypes method: a self-guided system for positive transformation, inspired by the work of Dr. Cowan, that utilizes the ancient wisdom of the Five Elements to create perpetual personal and interpersonal harmony and balance. By practicing this method, you'll become more aware of the patterns of repeated behavior that thwart efficacious potential, you'll learn simple techniques to re-center in the face of stress, and you'll gain a strengthened sense of personal clarity so that you can make better, more growth-focused decisions in your personal and professional life.

WHY I WROTE THIS BOOK

I was twenty-one years old when my father passed. When I resurrect the memories of that short sliver of time, I observe them as dappled, staccato, clear images—kind of like billboards I once glimpsed that left a distinct mark on my brain. Among these images is the time when an older woman came to my grandmother's house to pay her respects after the funeral. She approached me with heavy-hearted eyes and said, "The Universe gives you only what you can handle. You must be one tough cookie." With that, my breath caught ice-cold in my chest and I burst into tears, burying my head in my mom's shoulder.

After the woman left, I continued to think about her "tough cookie" comment. Her perspective on my predicament didn't seem at all fair or right. I hated her suggestion, and I hated her for saying what I thought was a stupid thing during a time when I was most fragile. But, as is the case with most things in life, a dose of time and space away from the situation granted me a fresh perspective.

As I look back, that experience still remains steadfast in my mind. But now, instead of serving as a harbinger of raw emotions, it's an invitation to expand my capacity for understanding interpersonal interactions. Instead of animosity, I have compassion for the woman who offered her condolences. Her intentions were pure. My ability to remain resilient in the face of conflict after my dad passed was extremely low. I don't blame her. I'm not a victim. Instead, time has allowed me to reframe and learn from comments that pummeled my heart all those years ago.

I've been able to achieve this sense of compassion by recognizing a natural force that drives all growth and development. This force is consistent and reliable, and reveals itself in a deeper understanding of myself and others. It's as dependable as the sunrise and the changing of the seasons. This force is a guide that helps us better comprehend the life journey we're all on.

This is not to suggest that we shouldn't characterize horrific life circumstances as such. My personal revelation has more to do with what actions we take in the face of challenges when they come up (and in the face of people saying things with good intentions that land poorly). I propose here that we have three choices for how to respond to our challenges:

1. We can expand, learn something, and prosper through discord and heartbreak.
2. We can ignore it for a while and try to function.
3. We can sink into reactive states that have the potential to cause harm to ourselves and others, and perpetuate a gaping wound that will one day rear its ugly head and manifest in maladaptive ways that hold us back from living optimally.

I wrote this book as an invitation to consider living in choice #1.

The Five Archetypes method is a map and a driver of perpetual expansion in the face of difficulty. It's a tool to give you more self-control over how you rise and embolden your resolve in the face of suffering. It will also help you do the following:

+ Understand and notice the traits, needs, and qualities of each of the Five Archetypes, which will help you accurately predict your stress states.
+ Practice actions that harmonize the Five Archetypes within your nature, making you more resilient in the face of stress triggers.
+ Apply your Five Archetypes knowledge to your daily life to become kinder to yourself and more empathetic with others, which will vastly improve your relationships.

Over the past several years, I've grown more amazed by how the Five Archetypes guide, support, and even predict personal growth. I started using this method to help my clients at Tournesol make better-informed management decisions and heal relationship wounds with lovers, spouses, friends, and coworkers. I've also used this method to help people attract and retain clients and reframe old perceptions of festering problems into new perspectives on the possibility of efficacious growth. Ultimately, I've come to realize that this method addressed, put into perspective, and revealed the most benevolent path toward harmonious personal and interpersonal relationships, and that is why I want to share it with you.

GETTING STARTED WITH THE FIVE ARCHETYPES

The Five Archetypes is a primer on understanding what makes people tick, so you can subsequently have more successful interpersonal relationships and a deeper understanding of your own needs and behaviors.

Think back to the situation I described at the beginning of this introduction—what do you notice when you walk into an unfamiliar room? Well, allow the Five Archetypes to tell you.

They are:

+ The Wood Archetype ("The Trailblazer")
+ The Fire Archetype ("The Optimist")
+ The Earth Archetype ("The Caregiver")
+ The Metal Archetype ("The Architect")
+ The Water Archetype ("The Philosopher")

Here's what each may have experienced when they walked into that room:

+ **Wood:** "I bet I can make my way around this crowd in thirty minutes flat, motivate a good eighty percent of them to stay for Bill's stand-up routine, and still get to the gym by nine p.m."
+ **Fire:** "It feels fun in here. I'm going to introduce myself to the exciting-looking people over there. I bet they'd be into the story I want to tell about the hilarious mishap that went down at work today."
+ **Earth:** "Aw. That lady over there has nobody to talk to, and she seems so lonely. I'm going to make her a plate of appetizers and go sit with her so she has some company."
+ **Metal:** "I'm so grateful there's a place like this in town where people can mingle nicely. But I think the owners should've considered starting these mixers a little later in the evening so more people could come."
+ **Water:** "I'm going to go sit at that quiet table in the back, where I can take it all in without the distraction

of the activity near the food table. Being in this room makes me wonder how other communities use social gatherings to improve overall well-being. I bet there are some good books on that topic."

And here's what's typically behind each of the Five Archetypes' specific decisions to engage in conversation with other people:

- **Wood:** They talk to motivate or to propel you toward change.
- **Fire:** They talk to entertain you so you stay and enjoy the amusement.
- **Earth:** They talk to find out about you and how they can teach and/or support you.
- **Metal:** They speak at the right time, not out of turn.
- **Water:** They speak to explore deep and meaningful ideas and shy away from casual conversation.

Every human on the planet is an amalgamation of all five archetypes, as demonstrated through body-, cognitive-, and spiritual-level behaviors and tendencies. Our Wood characteristics motivate us to exercise and move through difficulty. Our Fire traits are behind our optimism and playfulness. Our Earth characteristics reveal themselves through our compassion and digestive health. Our Metal traits remind us to triple-check an email for proper punctuation and to breathe when we become frustrated. Our Water traits call upon us to pause, listen, and make sure we get good sleep.

While each of the Five Archetypes has distinct features, these variations serve an invaluable purpose. They interact with one another purposefully and seamlessly, serving as an intricate support system for human learning and expansion. We require a mix of influences in our lives to grow and learn new skills. Sometimes we need to feel irritated to remind us to pause and evaluate our current situation to discover what needs to change, and sometimes we want to be supported and nurtured so we can continue along our chosen path. At certain points, repeating trivial mistakes a few times is all we need to recognize that something we're doing needs to shift. Other times, it takes a considerably less pleasant event to alert us that it's time to evaluate and adjust our trajectory.

The Five Archetypes naturally provide all these influences. If you allow them to, the traits and skills of each will either motivate, exasperate, or calm you, as well as direct you toward a path for improvement. When you understand the archetypes' associated behaviors and how they interact, you can more easily stay the course of learning and growth in the face of challenge. You'll be able to predict potential pitfalls and stress states by building a customized road map for self-awareness and recovery from disappointment. Additionally, the more familiar you become with the Five Archetypes, the more intimately you will understand and empathize with other people's journeys, resulting in improved empathy and relationships with others.

This strategy for growth is what I have learned and continue to learn from Dr. Cowan. He reminds me that being in a state of growth is heroic, even and especially when growing feels uncomfortable.

♦ ♦ ♦ ♦ ♦

"Carey, tell me, how long is mastering the Five Archetypes method going to take?"

I hear this question a lot. I ask it myself. *How long do I have to suffer in this stress state and with these problems? Make it all go away—and fast!*

Many conversations I have had with Dr. Cowan, dissecting and investigating human behavior, recent research, and modern trends, loop back to and land on this topic. We are a society that views discomfort as something to eradicate rather than something to evaluate. We run from distress, and we don't tolerate hardship, uneasiness, or pain well. I'm not suggesting we allow people to live in agony; rather, I'm inviting you to consider that the onset of a challenge could be an opportunity to evaluate and assuage its fundamental source.

The words on these pages are all just marks and dashes, information and entertainment. The magic is in how you transform the ink on this paper into knowledge through the creation and practice of new habits in your own life. This transformation of which I speak has no time limit or expiration date. Would you stop exercising as soon as your BMI reached your desired point? Would you stop eating food that nourishes your body and mind because you felt good on one particular day? Would you not water your garden again because it looked just perfect for a moment? Of course you wouldn't.

The "how long is this going to take" question is a bit of a trap. So is the "why is this happening to me" question. The Five Archetypes method asks you to consider reframing these questions instead. Rather than "How long" and "Why me," consider asking, "What?"

- ✦ What am I feeling?
- ✦ What factors are contributing to these feelings?
- ✦ What do I need right now?
- ✦ What work do I need to do for myself to feel less triggered by these situations?

"How long" and "why" are temporary and limiting questions, cutting you off from possibility. "What" means that you're open to exploration; it encourages and empowers you to discover your own potential in this life. "What" puts you more in control of your destiny.

The Five Archetypes method outlined within these pages amplifies the courage to ask "what" and extends guidance to help you figure out the answers. It helps you observe your challenges with objectivity and pinpoint your spot along the trajectory of growth. This way you're aware of the journey ahead and the achievements you've realized, and you don't feel adrift in a sea of disillusionment. It helps you feel less lost in the weeds and more resolute in your vision of the way forward. It recharges your problem-solving batteries and propels you toward living a fulfilling life.

This is not a system of judging or valuing the worth of one archetype over another. It's a method for how to better care for yourself and others—a method that encourages you to explore and perceive everyone's unique gifts with wonder, appreciation, and compassion. Would a tree judge the sun or shun the rain? If it did, the tree wouldn't thrive. The Five Archetypes method reminds us that we thrive when we embrace the diverse experiences, thoughts, and perceptions that we encounter from all the archetypes as part of our daily journey. They are precisely the universal gifts that help us thrive and live in harmony with one another.

YOUR PRIMARY ARCHETYPE
AND YOUR FLUCTUATING NATURE

It bears repeating that we have all five of these archetypes within our nature. Their delicate and dexterous arrangement remains in a constant state of motion. This dynamic flow is influenced by the interrelationships among each of the five in response to the shifting internal and external context of every moment in our day. The Five Archetypes regulate and arouse each other naturally, just as the atmospheric pressure influences the fluctuations in the weather and the transforming display of clouds in the sky. However, even though all these types are present within us, the vast majority of us have one of these Five Archetypes that serves as our primary.

Your primary archetype is the lens through which you experience all the pleasures and challenges of life. It is the embodiment of your unique gifts in this world. It anchors and directs your specific, characteristic mannerisms. It represents your personal "rules of engagement" in social interactions. It drives the distinctive way you express your stress states and how you connect in personal and professional relationships. While you will use the life skills associated with all five archetypes throughout your daily interactions, your primary archetype supersedes the rest, fueling your motivations and defining your style of connecting to your world. For example, my primary archetype is Fire, which means I tend to seek the good in all people and situations. I'm naturally driven to inject joy into my interactions with others. I feel an innate sense of responsibility for reducing the amount of time people around me spend feeling sorrow. When I'm with clients, my inherent method of communication is cheerful and encouraging. I always greet people with a welcoming smile, drawing them in with gentle eye contact and sharing my optimism for a positive outcome.

Right now, you may be thinking, *How can someone's way of being be both fixed and constantly shifting?* Well, your primary archetype is "fixed" in that it defines the characteristic fashion in which you engage with your environment throughout your lifetime. You are also in a state of constant flux along your primary archetype's strength–stress spectrum, which is affected by how safe and resilient you feel in any given moment. So, for example, when I feel secure, my Fiery optimism has the potential to help people believe in a positive outcome. However, if I feel insecure and go overboard trying to prove myself, my stressed Fire can become overly optimistic or too cheery without a solid plan to back it up. As a result, my confidence falls flat, and people may not trust my ability to help them actualize their goals.

Knowing your primary archetype expands your capacity for self-awareness. It helps you understand what is uniquely fabulous about you, what you contribute to your relationships, and what you bring to society at large. At the same time, knowing which archetype is your primary illuminates specifically how you will manifest your archetype-based stress states in your physical body, in your thoughts, and with others. Your reactions to positive and negative stimuli are distinctive and rooted in your primary type. Your ability to cope with life's challenges depends upon how resilient you are, which is influenced by how well you understand and meet your archetype-based needs for balance and by how well harmonized the non-primary archetypes are within your nature. One of the things I find fascinating about this method is that once you know your primary, you are able to predict and avoid repeated and frustrating behavior patterns and interpersonal pitfalls.

While your primary archetype's aptitudes, aversions, and distinctive ways of engaging are fixed, you still exist within a state of fluidity along your strength–stress spectrum. From our tiniest cell to our most leviathan perceptions of our purpose on this planet, our bodies and minds are always in motion, propelled by our internal emotions and any number of external factors. Our point along our archetypal strength–stress spectrum at any given time is informed and impacted by a confluence of forces, including our level of mental stability, the context of the moment, the circumstances of our internal and external environments, our past experiences, our vision of the future, what we had for breakfast, and how well we cope in the face of disappointment.

As I pointed out with regard to my Fire, when your primary archetype is unbalanced, you can exhibit too much or too little of your "unique gift," like being excessively hopeful, overly empathetic, or too quiet. Under these circumstances, you won't feel good. Physical, emotional, and spiritual unease escalates, and you won't enjoy your life all that much. However, when you know what internal signs to look out for, you begin to recognize and even predict your stress states before they creep up and cause discomfort. You'll also be able to stave off potentially explosive internal and external interactions down the road. With this deeper awareness, you essentially become the master of your domain (although not in the *Seinfeld* way!). As a master, you feel stronger, healthier, more empowered, and grounded. Inside your body, you have less cortisol pulsing through your system and are better able to face life's daily challenges. In relationships, you become a sage, a teacher, an example of an existence in which compassion, vulnerability, and self-reflectiveness serve as tokens of wisdom and groundedness in all your interactions both at home and at work.

When you're in touch with your needs and those of the people around you, the way you experience life is forever elevated.

✦ ✦ ✦ ✦ ✦

Having worked closely with the Five Archetypes method for several years now, I'm able to recognize and regulate my stressed Fire panic and overly excited energy more quickly. Sometimes, when I'm working with people who are uncomfortable around a boisterous Fire presence, I adjust my level of liveliness out of empathy for their discomfort. Now I'm able to shift my style of engagement to the point that those around me have no idea my primary archetype is Fire. To do this, I call upon my challenger archetypes, Metal and Water (see page 4), to help temper my blaze so that others feel at ease around me. My primary Fire can be off-putting when it's burning too bright, especially to Water and Metal types. To show compassion for the needs of others, I acknowledge and empathize with their sensitivity to Fire behaviors. Instead of assuming everyone loves to be entertained, I choose interactive styles that help everyone around me feel secure, so they have an easier time trusting me and learning from me, as well as sharing with me and being vulnerable.

Again, at any given point in time, you are an intricate and deliberate mix of all five archetypes. Even though you are essentially motivated by the qualities of your primary, you need all of the Five Archetypes to proceed effectively through your day-to-day life because each provides a specific skill to help you navigate any situation.

+ Your Wood helps you make sure all your students are lined up and out of the classroom on time during a fire drill at school.

- Your Fire helps you cheer up a friend who's feeling down.
- Your Earth helps you engage in a conversation with the new guy at the office so that he feels welcome.
- Your Metal allows you to perfect the proposal you're writing before turning it in.
- Your Water enables you to quiet your mind and see a complex problem from a different perspective.

THE FIVE ARCHETYPES AND EMPATHY

One of the many outcomes of achieving harmony among the Five Archetypes within your nature is the development of a reliable sense of empathy toward yourself and others. When you live with empathy at the center of your intentions and interactions, you acquire highly adaptive skills for well-functioning relationships.

Many minds have examined the importance of empathy over the years. Mystics, poets, sociologists, psychologists, neurologists, clergy, and laymen alike have dissected its meaning and displayed the multifaceted benefits of infusing our lives with empathy. Persian mysticism likens empathy to a spirit of universal connectivity that runs through all beings, a single consciousness to which we all belong, indistinguishable from one another.[1] James Baldwin, the American playwright and novelist, acknowledged that empathy offered a modicum of relief from heartbreak and pain upon realizing that his experience of torment in his life meant he was connected with and bound to "all the people who were alive, who had ever been alive." Psychologist Daniel Goleman differentiates among three types of empathy. He identifies them as "cognitive empathy," the ability to

---

1   Sumit Paul, "Empathy, the Essence of Persian Mysticism," *Times of India Blog*, accessed April 27, 2019, https://timesofindia.indiatimes.com/blogs/toi-edit-page/empathy-the-essence-of-persian-mysticism/.

see the world through someone else's eyes; "emotional empathy," tuning in so closely to another person that you can feel what they feel; and "empathic concern," which is the action of connecting when we express caring about another person.[2]

Compared to the Five Archetypes paradigm, Goleman's emotional empathy is most closely related to Fire's natural proclivity for intuitively feeling other people's emotions. His cognitive empathy corresponds to the overall wisdom you gain as a by-product of understanding and practicing empathizing with the needs of each of the five types in your daily interactions over time. Goleman's empathic concern correlates to the Earth type. It's the choice we make in the moment to actively show concern for someone else's well-being and to share with them what they need to feel better.

The skill of empathy requires that we deeply understand ourselves and others without judgment. So, as empathizers, we are also curious spectators. We are interested in knowing how other people live. It's both fascinating and perplexing to discover what people do with their time. We preoccupy ourselves marveling over what may have led someone to live in a tree, on a farm, or in a high-rise apartment building. We fantasize about what it might be like to live out life in someone else's circumstances.

What makes each of us tick? What makes some people stay in one relationship for a lifetime and others strive for perpetual single-dom? Why do some people seem to adhere to specific healthy lifestyle choices while others try out a new technique every few days? Why do some people believe everything you tell them and others, conversely, make you prove it? Why do people who seem to have the same life experiences develop radically different habits, tendencies, likes, dislikes, and abilities, and how do we use this awareness to constantly improve our lives and our relationships?

That is what this book will tell you.

---

2   Daniel Goleman, "Empathy 101," DanielGoleman.info, accessed October 13, 2013, http://www.danielgoleman.info/empathy-101/.

The Five Archetypes doesn't merely describe different personality types. It's an owner's manual and life strategy for recognizing, embracing, and celebrating the natural power of who you are. It outlines a method for refining your unique constitutional abilities so they can serve as a beacon of emboldened strength inside you and for those around you. The gift of the Five Archetypes is a simple system to help you build and sustain three key factors that reinforce better well-being outcomes and high-functioning relationships. These are:

+ Self-awareness
+ Self-regulation
+ Compassion

The more awareness and control you have over your responses to stress, the less time you'll spend in discomfort during life's challenging situations.

Keep in mind that this is not a one-and-done system of instant recovery from setbacks. Instead, this compassionate practice is a way of life. Imagine that achieving and embodying compassion is akin to the rhythmic repetition of breathing. *Be* compassion. Check in with your internal compassion barometer the same way you gauge your hunger. Make it part of how you do your day, and it will become as familiar as the way you take your coffee.

The Five Archetypes method can be applied to anyone, to any life situation, and at any time in one's life cycle. This book should serve as a guide you can pick up and utilize to better understand your feelings, fears, and tendencies and those of the people you encounter in your private and professional life every day.

CULTIVATE A FERTILE FOUNDATION FOR PRACTICING THE FIVE ARCHETYPES METHOD

Imagine that you set out to plant a garden. How would you prepare and create the most favorable environment, one that ensures your bounty has the best chance of success?

To start, you'd probably research the best plants for your environment. Then you'd choose the spot for planting that has the best sunlight. You'd likely evaluate and then bolster the soil with fertilizer. You'd till the ground and plant the healthiest seeds. Committed to a flourishing garden, you'd nurture your plants over time with the right combination of sustenance, love, and attention.

Having put your heart into this garden, you appreciate how your investment in preparation, your focused attention, and your consistent work paid off. Before you know it, you're enjoying the literal fruits (and vegetables) of your labor. Your devotion over these months of cultivation was packed with love and cemented a strong sense of connection, diligence, and pride in your accomplishments.

I want you to plant and tend to the perpetual garden of your blissful life. Just as you would research methods and prepare your land to yield an abundant harvest, I've written this book to help you prepare yourself for cultivating a flourishing personal and interpersonal garden of success.

Prepare first by making a choice, a decision to explore a way of participating in life that perhaps you haven't explored before. The Five Archetypes method asks you to perform self-research by pausing and taking note of yourself in the moment a bit more often and with more attention than you're probably used to.

In the stillness of these reflective moments, you'll uncover previously hidden and intricately detailed insights. Like appreciating the magnificence in the glorious unfolding of a flower garden you have built and cared for, these gems of self-enlightenment become profoundly rewarding details that inform a ripening internal maturity throughout a lifetime.

We have easy access to information on how to prepare land for gardening, but there's not a lot out there about how to prepare and cultivate our mind and body for developing, ripening, and realizing a harmonious life. This book serves as a guide for your journey. But before you begin this journey, it's important to prepare your "soil" to ensure it yields consistently healthful experiences.

In order to achieve growth and positive change through the Five Archetypes method, you must first familiarize yourself with the four phases of cultivating positive transformation. Practicing these phases will teach you self-evaluation, which opens the window to more precisely understanding why frustrating things happen and the amount of control you have over them. It's important for all of us to review and practice these four phases, especially when we are more inclined to blame others or to deflect accountability in conflict. These phases guide us to more effectively recognize, address, and resolve issues of inner instability. The more we believe in our capacity to control our own actions, the less time we'll spend feeling aggravated as a result of conflict.

The four phases to cultivating the groundwork for positive personal transformation are:

1. Get quiet and listen.
2. Track what comes up for you.
3. Plan ahead.
4. Actively integrate your more progressive wisdom each day.

First, you must practice pausing to observe the present moment. Literally "stop and smell the roses." Make an effort to sustain enough of a sense of *presence* throughout your day to *realize promptly when there's something wrong*. Many of us live in chronic states of stress and don't even know what it feels like to have peace, so it may take more concentrated focus to identify the subtle cues of disharmony.

We expend extraordinary energy each day distracted by thoughts and activities other than self-observation. For example, we may not realize how much time we spend trying too hard to fit in, win, or be right, or to escape the judgment and criticism of others. In Phase One, practice pausing and listening to these tendencies. Many of you will experience a fair amount of self-growth in Phase One just by deciding to push the proverbial pause button.

When you choose quiet and spend more time listening, your life comes alive with nuance, vibe, effervescence. It becomes gentler, softer, more reflective, less of a push-pull and more of a pleasing evolution forward with awareness and calm.

In Phase Two, you will pay close attention to and observe and track the details of your stress states. Keep in mind that it's important in Phase Two to consciously avoid judging yourself or any other people involved in the particular situation at hand. If you find yourself casting judgment while you're tracking your stress symptoms, track that tendency as well.

Through taking the time to observe these details, the world becomes enriched before you. Subtle distinctions that reveal layers of meaning and beauty expose themselves like a magnificent painting whose essence unfolds in phases as you quiet yourself enough to truly appreciate the meaning and intention of the artist.

Here's what to track in this phase:

1. Pay attention to the first signs of anxiety in your body. Physical expressions of stress manifest differently for each of us. You may notice things like shallow breathing, increased heart rate, sweating, numbness, prickliness, body tension, racing thoughts, or negative internal chatter. Merely identifying the connection between your emotions and your body's reaction to them can help temper the swell of intensified feelings. You may feel the urge to react to these feelings, but hang tight. From a

Five Archetypes perspective, these somatic signals are the body's way of asking you to pause and begin observing your surroundings.

2. Look around you. What are you aware of in the moment? Who is with you? What was just said? What are the details and circumstances that preceded your body telling you that your stress levels were elevated?

3. What are your personal circumstances? Did you sleep well last night? Did you skip breakfast? How many cups of coffee did you drink today? Are you hydrated? Did you have an argument with your best friend? Are you grieving a recent loss? What time and day is it? Tracking these details helps you recognize patterns in your stress triggers.

   These details of your personal circumstances impact your ability to be resilient in times of stress. After tracking for a few days, you may realize that you tend to forget to eat breakfast and then have less patience for coworkers around 11:00 a.m. These two clues combined beg a simple solution: Eat breakfast!

There's a broad context to the causation behind challenging feelings, and all of it matters when you're investigating your stress triggers and tendencies. Give yourself a gift by taking some time to identify your patterns. Empowered with this level of awareness, you are best prepared to initiate your foray into the Five Archetypes model for harmony and make positive, lasting change in your life.

When you are cognizant of disharmony in your mind and body and notice the broader complement of factors that impact your emotional states, you can then practice preparing and fortifying yourself in advance of situations you've come to realize feel prickly. For example, protect yourself with boundaries around how long you spend on the phone with challenging people by stating from the get-go that you have only five minutes to talk.

In Phase Three of cultivating the groundwork for positive transformation, just as in Phase Two, remember to recognize whether you begin to deflect or to blame others for your uncomfortable feelings. At this juncture, the more powerful transformative effort is around remaining in a self-reflective state, which admittedly can feel uncomfortable. But that's okay. Being self-reflective increases your ability to plan ahead for how you'll engage in difficult situations. Observe the discomfort that comes up and what it tells you about the self-regulation muscles you still need to strengthen. As a result, you'll begin to reimagine challenges as opportunities for building new life skills and spend more time in fulfilling relationships and activities.

Phase Four is when you bask in the fruits of your labor. You now have established a pretty reliable and fresh way of observing and addressing your challenges that has become integrated as a new habit. At this point, your brain has built a more fortuitous muscle that is now the norm for how you address formerly unpleasant situations.

In the end, these phases are about action, not just intention. Do the work in your mind first. Pay attention, track, and plan. But if you don't turn what you've learned into action, it's all just fantasy that doesn't actually improve your life. Bring it forth. Make it happen. You wouldn't be sustained by an imaginary garden, and you won't be fulfilled through intentions of love and connectivity that you don't implement.

✦ ✦ ✦ ✦ ✦

Sustained success using the Five Archetypes method requires patience, attention, and practice over time, but you won't have to wait long to notice progress. Once you simply become aware of your archetype-based individual needs, you're likely to begin experiencing a sense of relief. The knowledge that your seemingly erratic patterns of thought and behavior correlate to a time-tested, proven system of balance is comforting. Learning that there's a built-in path to fulfilling relationships within this method is even more reassuring.

Gaining self-knowledge through the rubric of the Five Archetypes results in a liberating realization that there's nothing intrinsically wrong with seeing the world through your unique brand of rose-colored glasses. Your remarkable, innate gifts are necessary to the propitious evolution of life on this planet. You'll also recognize that becoming stuck repeating patterns of ineffective thoughts and behavior is your archetypal nature reminding you to take a step back, evaluate your current challenge, and see what needs to be adjusted or improved for next time. Taking this awareness to heart is the beginning of taking your power back from the beliefs, people, and places where you may have left it along the way.

Most of us grapple with the age-old questions *Why am I here?* and *What's my purpose?* There are so many things about our future we can't foretell, like who will come into our lives to help shape our journey, the jobs we'll get, or the unexpected lessons we'll learn along the way. But this archetypal code does impart reliable wisdom and clarity that will make your life adventure much less turbulent. You'll learn to understand and predict how you intrinsically contribute to others' journeys and how they, in turn, impact yours. You'll begin to see clearly that we're all intertwined and interconnected. Once you know your nature and understand the nature of those around you, you are able to thrive, have your needs met, and navigate the challenges along your life path with ease. The dependability and consistency of this method ultimately provide a respite from the chaos and uncertainty of our modern life.

WHAT TO EXPECT
AND HOW TO USE THIS BOOK

The *Five Archetypes* is a guide to building more harmony in your life—whether with yourself or in your relationships. It's an invitation to become better at every internal and external interaction you have by becoming more aware of, and in control of, your behavioral tendencies and understanding of the people around you. When you're using this guide, I want you to remember that you are limitless. Your primary way of uplifting others, improving relationships, making things work better, creating systems, impacting a company, contributing to a team, or leading a movement—all are manifested through your own unique and beautiful brand of brilliance. Celebrate it! Teach it to others with a generous spirit, and learn how to deeply care for the lessons you learn from all the other archetype teachers in your life.

One of the first things you can expect to learn from this book is that each of the Five Archetypes demonstrates a unique set of gifts that can manifest as strengths or as stress states. For example, the Metal gift of creating beauty and consistency is necessary for living a balanced life. But this gift can become stifling to others if Metal isn't able to counterbalance this ability with the flexibility to take other people's opinions into account. That being said, your position along your stress—strength spectrum is constantly shifting as a result of a confluence of factors, including:

- Environmental (internal/external)
  - Did you sleep well last night?
  - Are important projects not going as planned?
  - Did you miss your train to work?
  - Are you in a fight with your best friend?
  - Do you have a headache or stomachache?
- The context of the challenging situation at hand
- Your individual archetypal nature

Once you understand the influence your nature, your environment, and your situational context have on your overall well-being, you can harness that knowledge and spend more time in courage, joy, compassion, and strength.

✦ ✦ ✦ ✦ ✦

Immediately following this chapter, you will find the Five Archetypes assessment. Your assessment results will illuminate your primary archetype as well as the order in which the other four fall within your nature. Your primary archetype reveals your characteristic traits and tendencies in strength and in stress. Your primary archetype also reveals that the particular way you manifest stress is naturally predetermined. This knowledge will give you the power to redirect the trajectory of your life toward harmony and balance.

Understanding your lowest archetype will grant you insight into what competencies you can improve upon in order to feel more balanced when facing stressful situations. Additionally, learning where the other three archetypes settle within the range of all five will help you clearly understand which coping skills you probably already favor and more naturally reach for to self-soothe and modify your more intense reactions in the face of stress.

To summarize, knowing your primary archetype will equip you with:

+ Self-awareness skills for identifying your needs as well as your specific stress and strength states.
+ Empathy skills to better support others by being aware that your primary way of engagement makes some people feel safe and others feel insecure.

Knowing your lowest archetype will reveal to you:

+ Which skills and temperament styles may be more challenging for you to access in times of stress.
+ Which skills to practice for building resilience to stress.
+ What types of people may push your stress buttons.
+ What self-care practices you may naturally avoid but need to do more often.

Becoming aware of your primary and lowest archetypes is an important part of your growth process. The individual archetype chapters will show you how to spend more time feeling strong by keeping your primary archetype harmonized. The skills you develop and the knowledge you gain from learning your primary and lowest archetypes will reduce the impact of uncomfortable stress responses and help you develop stronger interpersonal relationship skills.

The archetypes that naturally nurture and challenge your primary archetype will also offer invaluable insight during your personal growth process. To determine your primary's supporting archetypes, flip back to the images of the elemental cycles on pages 3 and 4 and look at the two elements adjacent to your primary. The skills, behaviors, and people associated with the elements/archetypes to the left and right of your primary will feel more nurturing to you and easier to tolerate most of the time. They instinctively encourage you to reach your goals, and they help you feel soothed when things aren't going your way.

On the other hand, the people, behaviors, and skills associated with the elements/archetypes that oppose your primary will come off as more prickly and challenging. You need these opposing archetypes to achieve balance and be effective at work and in relationships, but you aren't likely to naturally gravitate toward them. In fact, the activities and people that correspond to your opposing archetypes will likely be those you shy away from and have to work harder to tolerate. These are your chronic button pushers, and empathizing with them can empower heroic states of resilience and compassion.

+ + + + +

In the individual archetype chapters that follow the assessment, you'll find the steps that are central to the Five Archetypes method. This method will teach you personalized skills for how to optimize your primary archetype with increased self-awareness and self-regulation skills, as well as how to achieve harmony in your life by increasing empathy for your own needs and those of others around you. In order to more effectively utilize the information in these archetype chapters, here are brief overviews of what the two main components of the Five Archetypes method entail:

OPTIMIZATION

Optimization is about gaining self-awareness and self-regulation. In the Five Archetypes method, optimization begins with identifying your primary archetype and then being mindful enough to recognize in the moment when you're in your primary type's coordinating strength and stress states. The act of recognizing calls upon your ability to adjust how you use your time. The optimization section in each archetype chapter will encourage you to take a conscious step back from the rigmarole instead of rushing through life, hoping that everything goes as planned. By simply learning and recognizing your primary archetype's stress and strength states, you will begin to have more control over them, which will make it easier for you to return to calm in the face of discomfort.

The next step toward achieving optimization is understanding your primary archetype's needs for safety. Knowing your unique needs will further expand your skill set for self-regulation. As you practice observing how you feel when your needs for safety aren't met, you begin to make the connection between your archetypal needs and the onset and subsequent severity of your stress states. This knowledge and mindfulness practice broadens your self-awareness and amplifies your ability to regulate in the face of difficulty.

HARMONIZATION

A harmonized life is not one that lacks stress and challenge. Harmonization as part of the Five Archetypes method is actually about achieving an elevated state of empathy, which leads to sustainable strength in the face of stressors and challenges. In harmony, you will be able to predict, avoid, and nimbly navigate the difficult personal and interpersonal moments of your own life. Simultaneously, harmony among your Five Archetypes will manifest as the power to support those around you whose primary way of engaging with the world may be naturally at odds with your own. In harmony, you have more tolerance and appreciation for people who usually push your buttons. At its core, a harmonized state of being is akin to unconditional love for yourself and those around you.

When your archetypes are harmonized, you notice the deeply meaningful interconnectedness within and throughout the global environment.

- You can clearly honor the deeper connections
  - between the food you eat and how you feel emotionally
  - between the sleep and exercise you get and the stamina you have
  - between your needs and those of the people in your life
  - between how you spend your time each day and your greater sense of purpose

THE FIVE ARCHETYPES AND RELATIONSHIPS

In addition to setting you on the path toward personal optimization and harmonization, this book will teach you how to recognize and foster more harmonious relationships with the following key people in your life:

- An employee/coworker
- A friend
- A romantic partner
- Your child

Relationships are where we test-drive what we think we know about ourselves and others. The intersection of me and you is where the magic happens. It's where I learn what's unique about me and how my beliefs and actions are received and reflected in your eyes, facial expressions, body language, and behaviors. It's the playing field of life, where we experiment with and practice our engagement tactics. It's the terrain where we are at the highest risk of having our hearts broken and simultaneously having the best shot of falling in delicious, lasting love. Where you and I meet is where we have the most potential to become heroes in this wondrous game of life.

We thrive in connectedness, affiliation, and socializing. In relationships, we exchange ideas, emotions, glances, intentions, and touches. We experiment to see what pushes his buttons and what calms her down. We learn how long we have to dig in our heels to get what we want. We find out what she likes to eat, and we examine what makes him feel safe. Together, we become the creators of life, literally and figuratively.

Applying your knowledge of the Five Archetypes to your relationships can increase your capacity to learn fascinating intricacies about yourself and others. As a result, you can develop exponentially expanded skills for empathy, listening, critical thinking, decision making, and compassionate communication, and therefore become a more reliable, stable, and predictable source of unconditional love for yourself and other people. The Five Archetypes method does *not* call for avoiding certain relationships because of your primary type or others' primary types. There are no inherently bad combinations based on our internal nature. Understanding relationships through the rubric of the Five Archetypes is about learning to achieve harmony within yourself so that you become a better partner to any of the five types while remaining present, aware, and empathetic to others.

A BRIEF NOTE BEFORE WORKING
ON YOUR RELATIONSHIPS

How did you learn to be successful in love and romantic relationships? Who taught you how to establish fortuitous connections with others in the workplace? Who gave you lessons on how to play nicely with your friends in the proverbial sandbox?

I think Relationships 101 should be a required class in school, but it's not. Yet.

One narrative that is passed down from mother to daughter and from friend to friend, and that has reverberated through television sets and screens in episodes of *Oprah* and Jada Pinkett Smith's *Red Table Talk*, is that you really must love yourself and work on yourself before you can truly show up as a stable partner in friendship and love.

As frustrating as it is to hear that, when all you want is to have reliable and earnest friendships and romantic partners, it is absolutely true. Before you can explore the intricate intertwining of your personality with someone else's and emerge victorious, it's best to show up knowing yourself and feeling strong. But what is the definition of a strong person? How do you know when you're adequately strong and ready for a sound friendship or an intimate relationship? Neha Chawla, MA, ATR-BC, LCAT, LP, FIPA, a darned good integrative psychotherapist and fellow of the International Psychoanalytical Association, has helped me a lot with these questions.

Neha is a dear friend and a brilliant therapist who dexterously leads people through murky waters to higher, more stable ground. She notes, "Working on our relationship with ourselves with honesty and authenticity ideally needs to precede the emotional work we do with others." Neha lists the qualities of people who are ready to delve into healthy relationships; they're:

+ Receptive to growth
+ Naturally self-reflective and mindful
+ Self-observing
+ Compassionate and empathetic

+ Resilient enough to self-regulate and utilize rationality and avoid judgment when triggered

Imagine the level of satisfaction around the world if we all entered into relationships possessing these qualities.

Relationships add a whole new dimension of complexity to one's self-awareness. As Neha believes, the ultimate goal of enhancing and maintaining self-awareness and self-reliance *within* relationship exploration is to decrease conflict and create greater resilience by strengthening communication between those involved. According to Neha, "How we relate to ourselves—our capacity for self-reflection, mindfulness, self-observation, and self-understanding with compassion and without harsh judgment—is extremely important to nurture and cultivate, because that is how we will most likely relate to others and the world that contains us." As Neha points out, healthy love and companionship starts with you. How well you know yourself and your temperament, and how well you can reconcile stress states, is directly related to how well you function with friends, lovers, coworkers, and clients.

Neha asserts that when you invest in knowing yourself with patience, honesty, and sincerity, you are more likely to have the clarity and grounding to observe the highly complex dynamics of relationships from a more compassionate and less agitated space. Additionally, through this work, people become more self-assured than aggressive, protecting their own needs while still empathizing with the needs of others.

To prepare yourself for the most gratifying relationship outcomes, you really have to commit to the understanding that building self- and interpersonal regulation and control is an essential component of a fulfilling life. Avoiding being mindful of your emotional and behavioral tendencies or choosing to ride the waves of what feels good in the moment without understanding your temperamental pitfalls has the potential to land you in an unpleasant relationship conundrum from which you have to dreadfully disentangle. It's not fun, and it's often avoidable. Because of this, Neha has a list of crucial actions that prepare us for successful bonds with others. She believes that by adopting these behaviors, we become more self-aware, compassionate, and resilient beings—and better able to engage in gratifying relationships.

These ongoing attitudes and behaviors are as follows:

+ Self-understanding from the perspective of our past, present, and anticipated future
+ Commitment to continually develop our strengths
+ Understanding our limitations
+ Becoming aware of our temperaments
+ Exploring our vulnerabilities
+ Examining our dreams, hopes, and fantasies
+ Getting to know our fears and triggers

At the end of the individual archetype chapters in this book, I touch upon the unique tendencies of each archetype within different kinds of relationships. But as you continue to learn about how the Five Archetypes interact with one another, I implore you to get to know yourself well first by becoming more deeply aware of your primary archetype and following Neha's advice. Practice becoming the best you, and you will see that your newfound awareness will naturally help you foster more successful and compassionate relationships.

THE FIVE ARCHETYPES,
SELF-CARE, AND AYURVEDA

We've all heard the idea that we must put on our oxygen masks first before we can assist others—and it's true. We're not much use to someone else if we're depleted.

Self-care works best when it's customized to meet your individual needs. As you'll learn in this book, you're drawn to certain types of exercise, certain patterns of eating, and certain needs for sleep and social interaction based on your primary nature. One way to make sure your wellness plan works for you would be to seek the help of a professional health-care worker who is trained to customize self-care guidelines. There are many health coaches, integrative doctors, Ayurvedic nutritionists, and acupuncturists who are skilled in building individualized holistic care plans for their clients and patients. If you're just starting out on your wellness journey, though, this book also offers personalized wellness practices to complement all five archetypes.

In the archetype chapters, I include some overall approaches to self-care for each particular archetype, as well as Ayurvedic strategies that correspond to that type's specific needs for balance. Ayurveda is a science concerned with living an optimal and healthy life. It's considered to be the world's oldest known medical system, originating in India more than five thousand years ago; it's a personalized method of care that encompasses a vast array of lifestyle medicine, including yoga, pranayama (breathwork), nutrition, sleep, stress-reduction techniques, and more.

I'm including Ayurvedic well-being practices in this book because they jibe seamlessly with the Traditional Chinese Medicine philosophy of achieving harmony by learning and being aware of nature's rhythms in our daily lives. Specifically:

+ They are both focused on improving overall quality
  of life rather than focusing only on eradicating symptoms and disease.

+ They both employ a holistic mind, body, and spirit approach to health.
+ They both endeavor to return the body back to homeostasis, or harmony, which fortifies the physical and emotional immune systems.[3]

While there are differences between the two systems, both Ayurvedic medicine and TCM perceive the body as having energetic centers and pathways that correspond to a host of interrelated physical, emotional, and spiritual qualities. By focusing treatment along and within these energy lines and areas, as well as on their correlating organ and endocrine systems and emotional and cognitive behaviors, the body and mind are supported and gently encouraged toward balance.

The energy centers associated with Ayurveda are called chakras, and Ayurveda identifies seven major chakras in the human body. From bottom to top they are:

+ Root Chakra
+ Sacral Chakra
+ Solar Plexus Chakra
+ Heart Chakra
+ Throat Chakra
+ Brow Chakra
+ Crown Chakra

According to Christopher R. Chase, MD, of the Department of Anesthesiology at the University of Vermont Medical Center and Larner

---

3   Bhushan Patwardhan, Dnyaneshwar Warude, P. Pushpangadan, and Narendra Bhatt, "Ayurveda and Traditional Chinese Medicine: A Comparative Overview," *Evidence-Based Complementary and Alternative Medicine* 2, no. 4 (December 2005): 465–73, https://www.ncbi.nlm.nih.gov/pmc/articles/PMC1297513/.

College of Medicine in Burlington, Vermont, the seven chakras share direct and specific correspondences to the Five Archetypes of TCM[4]:

+ Root Chakra: Water Archetype
+ Sacral Chakra: Earth Archetype
+ Solar Plexus Chakra: Earth Archetype
+ Heart Chakra: Fire Archetype
+ Throat Chakra: Metal Archetype
+ Brow Chakra: Wood Archetype
+ Crown Chakra: Fire Archetype

Boost your sense of agency by personalizing your self-care approach. Ayurveda and the Five Archetypes method are systems that empower you with customized well-being road maps. They each pair deep self-knowledge and understanding with natural strategies for balance. Practicing these methods will improve your skills for self-regulation in the moment and expand your foundation of resilience over time.

You will notice that the Ayurvedic lifestyle practice sections at the end of each archetype chapter provide a variety of multisensory self-care recommendations. This is because when we feel *dis*harmony in the mind or body, it's expressed throughout all our senses. Our ability to think, be creative, love, smell, taste, see clearly, listen, digest, sleep, stretch, move, feel emotions, hear ourselves or one another, and access our greater sense of purpose can all be impacted as a result of a spiritual, emotional, or physical imbalance. Ayurveda suggests that we can reestablish balance by using multimodal and multisensory therapeutic interventions. Therefore, the strategies listed in these sections endeavor to restore balance through our

---

4   Christopher R. Chase, "The Geometry of Emotions: Using Chakra Acupuncture and 5-Phase Theory to Describe Personality Archetypes for Clinical Use," *Medical Acupuncture* 30, no. 4 (August 1, 2018): 167–78, https://www.ncbi.nlm.nih.gov/pmc/articles /PMC6106753/.

different senses. They involve aromatherapy, color therapy, yoga, tastes, and sounds, and overall, they give us a greater understanding of personal strength and purpose.

Ayurveda, like the Five Archetypes method, provides insights into how to live in harmony with nature and natural rhythms. The practical guidelines of both systems can help us take control of our lives and culti-vate radiant health.

✦ ✦ ✦ ✦ ✦

In the archetype chapters of this book, you will also find information on how to optimize overall well-being according to each particular archetype. I encourage you to follow the advice you feel drawn to in the Ayurveda section that correlates to your primary archetype. That said, you may also consider following the Ayurvedic guidelines for the archetypes you want to enhance within your nature. Feel free to have fun and try the practices that speak to you.

As you peruse the Ayurveda and self-care sections, keep in mind that we are naturally drawn to strategies that match our primary archetype and repelled by those that represent our opposing archetypes, or those in which we scored the lowest on the assessment. Remain aware of how balanced a regimen you keep. Track the lifestyle improvements you avoid integrating and the ones you favor. To achieve harmony within yourself, you'll need to practice self-care activities that pertain to all five arche-types, not only the ones you like most.

Ultimately, my hope is that the Ayurveda and other self-care strate-gies in this book will expand your options for achieving and maintaining a sense of overall well-being.

✦ ✦ ✦ ✦ ✦

Personal and interpersonal struggles over our lifetime cause wounds that, when left unexamined, can intensify and impair our ability to experience a fulfilling life. We often wonder why we get stuck in ruts, repeating thought and behavior patterns that don't serve us. As time passes, we ache for some semblance of relief from the discomfort we feel. Without a seemingly simple "way out," we sometimes veer toward destructive activities and behaviors to feel better. The antidote is self-awareness. By becoming aware of who you are and what you need through the Five Archetypes method, you'll have unfettered access to the personalized tools and skills that will help you thrive.

Now that you have a better idea of the way in which the Five Archetypes method can help you build self-awareness, self-regulation, and empathy so that you can more effectively predict and overcome obstacles in personal and interpersonal relationships, you're ready to take the assessment and start using the guidelines that follow.

THE ASSESSMENT

The following assessment[5] is the result of decades of work conducted by Harriet Beinfield, LAc; Efrem Korngold, LAc, OMD; and Stephen Cowan, MD, although some of the statements in the assessment have been slightly modified to reflect my own experience with clients and how they tend to approach the phrases. I am humbled and honored that Harriet, Efrem, and Dr. Cowan have allowed me to use their work here to provide you with a time-tested and long-established tool for measuring the five types within your nature.

Using the scale on the following page, write down next to each phrase in the assessment the number that best represents your belief about how the phrase relates to you. When deciding on the number to choose, consider how frequently over the past three months you've felt or experienced the phrase in question. Imagine you're saying, "In the past three months, I would say that I . . ." before each phrase. With the recent past in mind, your answers will more accurately reflect a sense of where you are right

---

5 You can find a copy of Harriet and Efrem's full Self-Assessment Questionnaire in chapter 7 of their book *Between Heaven and Earth: A Guide to Chinese Medicine.* You may also opt to complete Dr. Cowan's five types questionnaire online at www .tournesol-assessment.com.

now and what Five Archetypes skills you need to work on in order to live a more harmonious life.

Be careful not to fall into the trap of "I should" when entering your answers. Sometimes people feel compelled to answer the "right" way, or the way they believe they truly should be thinking, as opposed to what is honestly true about themselves right now. To put yourself on the best path to optimization and harmonization through the Five Archetypes method, make sure your answers to the statements are sincere reflections of your authentic self right now.

Rate each statement on a scale of 0 through 4, as follows:

0: Never (totally not something I would do)
1: Seldom (maybe . . . but if so, I'd probably do it once every other week)
2: Sometimes (meh . . . once or twice per week probably)
3: Frequently (yeah, a lot of the time, but not always)
4: All the time (oh, that is *totally* me)

Tally your scores for each section on the "Total" lines that follow. Then record each of your five totals in the box on page 60, and make sure you match up the right total to the corresponding archetype. This is your Five Archetypes Summary, which represents the current state of balance of each of the five types within your nature.

Your highest total indicates your primary archetype, and it will likely remain your primary throughout your lifetime. However, your other totals could shift somewhat over the months and years, which is to be expected. Your ability to cope in the face of disappointment and to honor the diverse gifts of those in your life will increase the more you practice the Five Archetypes method, and as you become more compassionate and resilient over time, you may notice that your assessment results shift accordingly.

For example, when I first took the assessment a few years back, my

Fire was highest, Earth was second, Wood a distant third, and Metal and Water an even more distant fourth and fifth. This breakdown manifested at that particular time in my life as me being:

+ **High Fire/High Earth:** Overly concerned about making people happy and taking care of their needs.
+ **High Fire/Low Metal:** Feeling like saying "no" would make people not want to be friends with me.
+ **High Fire/Medium Wood/Low Metal:** More interested in making sure everyone was having fun than in getting my work done.
+ **High Fire/Low Water:** Uninterested in meditation of any kind because it wasn't fun or entertaining.
+ **High Fire/High Earth/Low Metal/Low Water:** Avoidant of too much due diligence prior to becoming involved with potential project collaborators because I didn't think it was nice or friendly to them.

Knowing my assessment results years ago gave me a distinct awareness of exactly what skills I needed to build for achieving balance among my Five Archetypes. Simply seeing my scores felt like a relief. I gained clarity on how the current state of the five types within my nature contributed to my often being more concerned about people liking me than about setting healthy boundaries. Additionally, my assessment results led me to the precise directions for how to create more healthy tendencies through self-awareness and archetype-based activities. As a result of personalized self-focus and a shift in behaviors, I became more consistently stabilized and made better decisions in my personal and work life.

These days, my scores fall in the same order they did the first time I took the assessment. However, my Fire and Earth are not that much higher than the other three, and my Wood score has increased so it is just a bit lower than my Fire and Earth. My Water and Metal remain my lowest two archetypes, but they have increased significantly, and there's less of a gap between them and my Fire.

The change in my scores manifests in my daily life in a few ways.

+ Metal improvement and calmed Fire: I'm still welcoming and friendly to those around me, but I now ask the imperative business questions and set boundaries that protect me and my company before engaging in collaborative projects.

+ Water improvement and calmed Fire and Earth: I now meditate alone almost every morning (*almost...*). The structured moments of calm allow me to quiet my Fire need to rush and fix things quickly. Instead, I can more easily pause and problem solve with clarity and creativity.

+ Wood improvement and calmed Earth: I now move projects forward with more speed, spending less time getting stuck feeling anxious about whether my decisions are going to please everyone involved.

The Five Archetypes assessment is intended to help you get more in touch with how the archetypes manifest and interplay within your temperament. As I demonstrated above in my own breakdown of the types, the actual numerical results are less pertinent to how you'll use the recommendations in this book than is the scale they reveal of your highest to lowest archetypes.

If you're not sure how to rank some of the statements in the assessment, consider reviewing them with your friends, and ask what they recognize in you. Sometimes our friends and family notice quirks and idiosyncrasies that evade us.

When considering the most accurate responses to the items in the assessment, don't worry too much about getting the "right" answer. There is no right or wrong response. You feel what you feel when you feel it. Your responses will naturally be nuanced and modified by your current emotional, physical, and spiritual state of harmony in any given moment, so you may notice slight variations in your assessment scores depending upon your mood, the day of the week, or the time of day. These slight variations are natural. If you take the assessment more than once less than a few days apart, you should find that your primary and lowest numerical scores may fluctuate a small amount, but their rank as highest and lowest will likely remain unchanged. The middle three may show some variation as well, but they don't impact your work in this book toward optimization and harmony in as substantial a manner as the highest and lowest archetypes will.

✦ ✦ ✦ ✦ ✦

Okay, I think you're ready. Grab a pen or pencil and get started on your assessment. Have fun with it. This is an exciting time for you, because it's the gateway to a newfound sense of relief, empowerment, and resilience. Enjoy!

0–4	WOOD
	I love being active and exercising.
	I enjoy taking risks.
	I feel confident and act assertively.
	I seek challenges and enjoy the pressure of competition.
	I'm comfortable with conflict.
	I prefer to lead more than I like to follow others.
	I can be pushy and might call out and express my opinions brazenly.
	I love an adventure.
	Once I'm done with a project, I don't want to have to revisit or refine it. I'm ready for the next thing.
	I take pride in being first, best, fastest.
	I hate losing.
	I learn by doing instead of talking about it.
	I'm not afraid of danger or uncertainty.
	I'm comfortable acting boldly and decisively, regardless of what others say or think.
	I acclimate quickly to new environments and circumstances.
	I tend to become restless and impatient with people I think are holding me back.

	I'm not swayed when a colleague says no to me about a work idea or plan. I believe "no" just means "not yet." I make things happen.
	I tend to blame others.
	I like to question authority.
	I tend to get tense and angry easily, and I shout when I'm stressed.
	I feel an urgency to disagree or argue with others' opinions, especially of me.
	I openly discuss my abilities and achievements.
	I'm reluctant to acknowledge other people's opinions, ideas, perspectives.
	I act quickly and decisively in a crisis situation.
	I enjoy standing up to injustices in the world as I see it.
Total:	

O – 4	FIRE
	I look for excitement and stimulation.
	I love to have fun, and others think I'm delightful to be around.
	I tend to feel my emotions and reactions intensely.
	I seek out ways to stay busy because I don't like being bored.
	I'm naturally very intuitive about what others think and feel.
	I can be gullible and easily believe what others say about me, the good and the bad.
	I'm very passionate about things I like.
	I'm animated and cheerful when I'm very excited about something and can jump, shake, or move my body without control.
	I can depend on my charm to get what I want.
	I like to cheer others up and to inspire others, because I don't like it when anyone feels sad.
	I love it when people notice, recognize, and reward me for things I've done.
	I'm optimistic and hopeful no matter what the situation or other people's opinions.
	It's easy for me to bounce back quickly after being upset because I don't like how it feels to be sad.

	When something upsets me, I tend to be oversensitive and melodramatic, and my anxiety and panic escalate quickly.
	I tend to avoid doing activities I don't think are fun.
	I can get bored easily.
	I enjoy eating for pleasure.
	I enjoy and need regular physical contact and emotional intimacy.
	It's easy for me to share my deepest feelings and desires.
	It's easy for me to focus on the present instead of worrying about the past or the future.
	I can easily see the humor in almost any situation.
	I become deeply identified with and responsive to the feelings, thoughts, and experiences of another.
	I am comfortable receiving and showing unabashed affection, enthusiasm, and excitement toward others.
	I enjoy being attractive and irresistible to others.
	I'm not afraid of being vulnerable in front of other people.
Total:	

O–4	EARTH
	I love socializing with friends and family.
	I'm naturally drawn to finding ways to resolve conflict among people.
	I don't like people not getting along.
	I'm very concerned about making sure I please others.
	I tend to be a loyal friend.
	People count on me to solve interpersonal and relationship problems.
	I feel comfortable with and am easily approachable to people I don't know well.
	It's easy for me to imagine what other people need.
	I'm considered a nurturer and will put others' needs before my own.
	I'm regarded as a team player.
	I like knowing others rely on me for help and comfort.
	I like being in relationships where I'm needed by my friends, family, and partner.
	I believe in the good intentions of others.
	I like fitting in.
	I don't want to be the leader or the center of attention.

	I tend to go along with what others say.	
	I don't like anyone being left out.	
	I like my home to be the central gathering point for friends and family to hang out.	
	I'm trustworthy and accessible.	
	I like to tell and listen to stories.	
	I can become indecisive, needy, and worried when stressed.	
	I tend to get stomachaches when I'm nervous.	
	I tend to have a hard time falling asleep when I'm overwhelmed or worried.	
	I can be shy in unpredictable social situations.	
	I can talk too much when I want people around me to feel comfortable.	
Total:		

O–4	METAL
	I revere people who have put in years of hard work and training to legitimately attain positions of esteem.
	I'm good at noticing details and patterns.
	I have a specific way to do things.
	I like being in control of situations.
	I feel secure when I know that everyone is following proper standards, principles, and expectations.
	I have high expectations of myself and others.
	I'm strongly committed to my moral values, principles, and standards of conduct.
	I enjoy logical, analytical, and systematic approaches to problem solving.
	I prefer consistency in my life and am averse to change.
	I tend to be judgmental and critical.
	I prefer a neat and orderly lifestyle.
	I try to make things perfect.
	I have strong likes and dislikes.
	I keep my emotions in check and respond to joy and disappointment in a reserved fashion.
	I tend to get stuck on what's wrong instead of what's right.

	I tend to be a picky eater.	
	I enjoy organizing my space and have a sense of satisfaction when everything is in its place.	
	I dig my heels in deeper when I'm stressed, becoming rigid and fixated on being right.	
	I appreciate well-defined goals and instructions.	
	I'm committed to moral principles and behavior.	
	I have good taste and recognize good taste in others.	
	I incorporate "lessons learned" into my life to make sure I don't make the same error twice.	
	I believe that virtue is more important than pleasure.	
	I feel tense when things seem chaotic and don't run smoothly.	
	I tend to get stuck on the details when I'm stressed.	
Total:		

O–4	WATER
	I take my time getting to know people before starting relationships.
	I prefer having a handful of good friends that I see every once in a while.
	I'm objective and reasonable when faced with other people's histrionics and drama.
	I don't need to always be in a relationship.
	I like working alone more than collaborating as part of a team.
	I can be stubborn and headstrong.
	People find me hard to read.
	I'm imaginative and perceptive.
	I'm a seeker of knowledge and meaning.
	I love spending time just thinking about ideas, concepts, or people.
	I take my time reacting to situations and events instead of responding in a hasty rush.
	I don't like having to stick to someone else's schedule or timeline.
	I keep my private life to myself and am careful about what I reveal to others.
	I prefer to figure things out for myself.

	I don't like being the center of attention; I prefer remaining anonymous.
	I lose track of time.
	I don't mind being unconventional or eccentric.
	I often fear the worst.
	I often forget where I put things down, like my glasses, wallet, keys, phone, or shopping lists.
	I understand that things take time, so I don't give up easily when I'm solving problems or creating new concepts and ideas.
	People say I'm more of a realist than an optimist.
	I need and cherish my alone time.
	I tend to withdraw and shut down, and I don't want to talk when I'm stressed.
	I can get lost in my imagination.
	I can get so caught up in a book, movie, or activity at night that I'll forget to go to sleep.
Total:	

FIVE ARCHETYPES SUMMARY

The Wood Archetype/The Trailblazer: _____

The Fire Archetype/The Optimist: _____

The Earth Archetype/The Caregiver: _____

The Metal Archetype/The Architect: _____

The Water Archetype/The Philosopher: _____

With your assessment result numbers in front of you, identify the scale of highest to lowest archetypes within your nature.

+ Your primary archetype is the one with the highest score.
+ Your secondary archetype is the one with the second-highest score.
+ Your third archetype is the one with the third-highest score.
+ Your fourth archetype is the one with the fourth-highest score.
+ Your lowest archetype is the one with the lowest score.

POSSIBLE ASSESSMENT OUTCOMES

You Could Have More Than One Primary

Some of you may have two, or even three, archetypes that are tied for your highest score. If that's the case, then congratulations are in order! You are naturally great at two or three different fundamental skill sets.

If you fall within this category, begin your journey by reading the sections on each of your primary archetypes so you can become universally more self-aware and understand the strategies for self-care that will apply to you in the context of different situations. As a dual (or triple) primary, you'll have divergent needs for safety at times, so becoming fluent in all your primary archetypes will help you become more resilient more of the time.

VERIFYING YOUR PRIMARY

If you happen to feel uncertain about whether your results correctly identified your primary archetype, there are a few ways to confirm your results. One way is to spend the course of a week closely paying attention to these three things about yourself:

1. What you're knee-jerk good at. (This corresponds directly to your primary.)

2. What you're like when you're upset and not able to easily access your composure. (This also corresponds directly to your primary.)

3. What sort of challenges and people push your buttons the most. (Refer back to the statements and tendencies in the assessment so you become more familiar with which behaviors correspond to each potential button pusher.)

For example:
- If Wood pushes you the most, you're more likely to have Earth as your primary.
- If Fire pushes you the most, you're more likely to have Metal as your primary.
- If Earth pushes you the most, you're more likely to have Water as your primary.
- If Metal pushes you the most, you're more likely to have Wood as your primary.

♦ If Water pushes you the most, you're more likely to have Fire as your primary.

If you still feel unsure about your results, take some more time to self-evaluate and gain certainty that you've correctly identified your primary archetype. As you know, your given pathway through this book toward living a harmonious life begins with the nature you've identified as your primary, so it's important that your results be correct. The firm awareness of your primary type can become even more obvious to you through paying attention to the details and context of your everyday life experiences. Observe and track your behaviors during even your most mundane movements throughout the day. Allow yourself some extra time to take in how you react and how you feel in response to interactions, setbacks, and achievements.

Highest Scores That Are Very Close

The assessment is quite thorough and sensitive. Even a tiny difference between your highest and your secondary archetypes connotes a significant enough differentiation to highlight the higher of the two as your primary.

However, if you're not positive, give yourself a week to observe your thoughts, reactions, and behaviors from the perspective of these two highest archetypes. Take note of your tendencies under stress, how you respond to good news, the types of people you're drawn to, and the types you're inclined to avoid. This is an exercise in gathering research for self-evaluation. With your new data in hand, retake the assessment, and see if you come out with a more obvious front-runner archetype.

If your scores remain just as close after your week of observation, then your highest score should be treated as your primary archetype and your second-highest as your secondary archetype. You'll follow the plan for creating harmony that correlates to your primary archetype.

Non-Primary/Supporting Scores That Are Very Close

Many of you will have non-primary scores that are very close, if not identical to each other. This outcome doesn't have a material impact on your work for creating harmony.

HOW TO USE YOUR ASSESSMENT RESULTS

Your Five Archetypes journey begins by strengthening your self-awareness. You'll achieve this by reading the chapter that correlates with your primary archetype(s) and then reading the chapter that corresponds to your lowest archetype. Diving into these two chapters first will help you get to know your primary ways and motivations, as well as highlight the characteristics you need to bolster in order to safeguard you from slipping into overactive or distorted primary archetype behaviors, such as being:

+ **Wood:** Too pushy, as opposed to empathetically coaching everyone along.
+ **Fire:** Too silly, as opposed to inspiring a balanced sense of optimism that everything will turn out all right.
+ **Earth:** Caring too much about others, as opposed to making sure your needs are met as well.
+ **Metal:** Too focused on upholding your own standards of perfection, as opposed to considering other people's perspectives.

+ **Water:** Too quiet and solitary in your imagination, as opposed to sharing new ideas and inventions with others.

Once you become more aware of your natural archetypal inclinations, you can begin to focus on the balancing activities listed in your primary archetype chapter. The activity sections are meant as a guide to help enhance your self-regulation skills and can be found on the following pages:

+ Wood: page 81
+ Fire: page 126
+ Earth: page 168
+ Metal: page 210
+ Water: page 253

Finally, to further expand your awareness and amplify your empathy and compassion for yourself and others, harmonize your Five Archetypes by reading the chapters that correlate to your middle three types. Then you will be able to broaden your understanding of your inclinations and become more familiar with how others in your life experience you and interpret their world.

WOOD

THE TRAILBLAZER

If you scored highest in Wood traits on your assessment and have confirmed that your results are accurate, then Wood is your primary archetype.

When Wood is your primary archetype, your bold determination directs the way you interact with your environment. You share the gifts of perseverance, grit, independence, and freedom with the world.

Primary Woods are the first people in line to explore unchartered territory. They'll show up at the airport on a Friday afternoon with no luggage, eager to choose a flight for an unplanned weekend adventure. They're the quarterback who relentlessly drives the ball down the field, nimbly cascading past every obstacle in his way until he reaches the goal. Wood types can also be the coach of the high school basketball team who stands by his team through thick and thin, refusing to give up on his players. He pushes them forward when the score tips in the competition's favor and reminds them with gusto that they can do this!

Wood is the desire to dive headfirst into a heated debate on a controversial topic and the moxie to defend a position when challenged. Wood is about not giving up, especially in the face of difficulty.

Primary Wood types motivate you and fuel your ideas until they come to fruition. They focus more on getting things done quickly rather than perfectly, but Woods know how to get you moving when you feel immobilized by worry or fear.

Also considered to be the "advocates" in friendships, Wood types make sure you're protected and mentor you to become strong and self-reliant. Seeing you succeed is deeply satisfying to them and emboldens their own sense of self-worth.

The Wood archetype, also known as "The Trailblazer," is associated with leadership, self-determination, and perseverance, meaning that people who are primary Woods will often seek out challenges and enjoy them, as well as perform well under pressure. On the flip side, their typical lifestyle challenges revolve around learning to appreciate the value in pausing and taking the time to nurture a plan or an idea and overcoming the frustration of feeling restricted in their pursuits, perspectives, and convictions.

Even if Wood is not your primary archetype, you will still have some amount of Wood in your nature, so in order to achieve and maintain harmony throughout your lifetime, take note of where your Wood ranks among the other four archetypes and practice the skills that help keep the Wood in your nature strong. The long-term maintenance practices beginning on page 85 will help you both optimize your primary archetype and harmonize, as well as provide a firm foundation of resilience in the face of stress. If Wood is your primary, practicing your long-term maintenance activities will naturally allow you to more easily pause in the face of quickly escalating feelings of anger when you're stressed and will increase your ability to move forward with goals and projects. If

Wood is your lowest, practicing these activities will naturally help you curb self-defeating thoughts and empower you with more drive to push through difficulties.

When Wood Is Your Primary Archetype

If Wood is your primary or is tied as one of your primaries, then this chapter applies most directly to you.

As a primary Wood, your enthusiasm to achieve higher heights and explore uncharted territory is unmatched. You have unencumbered access to bravery and gumption. When you're on top of your game, your friends, family, and community regard you as the courageous one to turn to when something needs to get done. You're a survivor, pushing forward to reach goals regardless of obstacles and consistently encouraging those around you to do the same.

Primary Wood types live their highest spiritual purpose through teaching and coaching others to realize their own ambitions. With fastidious care and sustained attention, they engage with others to encourage them on their chosen path to success. They demonstrate how to move through real and perceived obstacles along life's journey. Wood types at their absolute best also want to express to others that spending time focusing on what's wrong instead of what's possible can hold you back from living a great life. Woods hope that, as a result of these efforts, others will begin to model the ability to push through negative thinking and attain their dreams by emulating what the Wood archetype illustrates for them.

Primary Wood types who feel grounded, self-aware, and secure in who they are will embody distinct traits in their physical, mental, and spiritual being. Physically, Wood types appreciate and enjoy regular exercise. Mentally, Wood types are excellent at planning and achieving goals. Spiritually, Wood types embody and share the gift of freedom to choose compassion even when tensions are high and emotions are difficult to control.

When your primary archetype is Wood, you'll exhibit specific inherent capabilities and attitudes. These patterns persist and are expressed in your personal behaviors, the self-care activities you favor, and the way others perceive you.

Here are some basic Wood archetype indicators to be aware of: When feeling resilient, a primary Wood is a survivor, pushing forward to reach goals, regardless of obstacles, and consistently encouraging those around her to do the same. On the other hand, when feeling insecure, the Wood type experiences strong feelings of frustration and anger and becomes acutely sensitive to criticism.

This is why it's important for Woods to recognize when it's time to self-regulate, rather than react in a maladaptive manner when faced with challenge. Sometimes we become so caught up in our dysfunctional thoughts and belief patterns that we can't easily distinguish between rightful action and reactive behavior. To help them make that distinction and more quickly notice reactive thoughts and behaviors, primary Wood archetypes should be on the lookout for times when they:

+ Get so engulfed in driving a project or idea forward quickly that they ignore their own self-care needs.
+ Care so much about other people's opinions of them that they get caught up in proving those attitudes wrong, and even begin to doubt themselves as a result of the perceived criticism.
+ Become very easily angered at even small things and have a hard time returning to a calm state (and/or are not aware of how their anger affects others).

The ultimate outcomes I hope you achieve as a result of practicing the Five Archetypes method as a primary Wood are twofold: self-empowerment and empathy for others. I want you to strengthen your personal resolve and know your unique brand of Wood-centered resilience so you can exercise it in the face of friction and conflict. When life's influences and forces lead you toward choices and behaviors that feel most Wood-type comfortable, like pushing your agenda without listening to others' feelings, I want to you have the awareness to pause and recognize that your comfort zone is not always your sacred path. With time and patience, you will establish a foundation of insight and understanding about how to maintain your Wood individuality while simultaneously empathizing with and meeting the needs of those around you.

When Wood Is Your Secondary Archetype

If Wood is your secondary archetype, it modifies your primary way of engaging in the world, meaning Wood behaviors and proclivities more often reveal themselves within your character than your lower three archetypal traits, but not as much as your primary traits.

For instance, as a secondary Wood, you may notice that Wood-specific challenges, such as impediments to moving quickly and unpleasant critiques of your work, can irk you intensely. These Wood-typical challenges won't chronically provoke you in the way that the ones associated with your primary will, but you will likely notice times when you have Wood needs you want met and Wood frustrations you seek to avoid. Arm yourself with the Wood knowledge in this chapter so you have access to Wood-balancing activities when the need arises.

Here are some archetype-based traits you may notice in yourself or others who are secondary Woods:

- Water with secondary Wood will have an easier time implementing their enlightened ideas in the world and in their relationships.
- Fire with secondary Wood cares greatly about maintaining friendships, but their gregariousness won't keep

them from pushing a potentially risky project forward with speed for fear of people liking them less.

+ Earth with secondary Wood cares a lot about enthusiastically helping you achieve your goals. They have the perseverance to follow through with you and make sure you succeed. Their need to please you will be mitigated by their secondary need to not get too stuck in the evaluating and planning stages of a project or relationship.

+ Metal with secondary Wood will create an organized and balanced strategy for carrying out big plans and will also make sure deadlines are met or even exceeded.

When Wood Is Your Lowest Archetype

Knowing that Wood is your lowest archetype sheds light on the archetype-based skills that may be harder for you to access overall. The scarcity of Wood will be more obvious to you in times of stress or when you feel stuck and unable to easily move past disappointment.

If Wood is your lowest archetype, you may not like to exercise regularly. You may also have difficulty envisioning a positive future resolution to your challenges, ranging from the most manageable to the more convoluted and gnarled of predicaments. With lowest Wood, speaking up for yourself can also be incredibly anxiety-inducing, so you may find yourself remaining in unpleasant situations longer than you'd like. Additionally, people who score lowest in Wood may spend more time panicking or overthinking their issues rather than moving quickly into outlining a strategy for solving them. Those with lowest Wood may also believe focusing on their own needs is improper, and they could have a difficult time sharing honest pride in their own achievements.

Having an awareness of your lowest archetype, however, can show you where you need to focus your energy so you can start building overall resilience to daily stress. Recognizing that Wood is your lowest archetype and doing the work to increase your Wood traits will propel you to build more rewarding interpersonal relationships, speak up for yourself when the need arises, and improve your ability to get out of situations that don't serve you.

THE FIVE ARCHETYPES METHOD

Optimization

The Five Archetypes method begins with optimization, a process that comprises three steps, which remain the same no matter which archetype is your primary. They are:

1. Recognize your primary archetype's strength and stress states.
2. Understand your primary archetype's individual needs for safety.
3. Achieve balance within your primary archetype.

As a result of optimizing your primary archetype, you will cultivate more empathy and compassion—for yourself and others—and replace old, ineffectual patterns with empowerment. You will embody stability and security in the face of upset. Optimization will also give you elegance and agility at times when you're feeling powerless or tossed about like a rudderless sailboat in response to unpredictable and unstable circumstances—and help you navigate those unchartered waters with more grace and stability.

Step One:
Recognizing Wood's Strength and Stress States

When your Wood archetype is balanced, you will notice that it contributes the strengths of perseverance, grit, independence, and freedom to your life, to your relationships, and to the broader community.

A balanced Wood also helps us:

- Nourish our bodies with exercise.
- Build strong muscles and stay fit.
- Implement our creative ideas.
- Make decisions instead of wavering for too long.
- Seek adventure and try new things.
- Not get too stuck in worry and overwhelm.
- Start over after a disappointment.
- Work hard to improve our skills.
- Become clear about what we want out of life.
- Stick with projects even when the going gets tough.
- Use our time more efficiently.
- Appreciate nature.
- Manifest our dreams.
- Formulate and stand by our opinions.
- Make plans and reach goals.
- Fight for what we believe in and not back down.
- Persuade others to join an organization or a cause.
- Maintain a diet or workout plan for the long haul.
- Encourage and coach others to constantly improve.
- Choose empathy over anger.
- Take well-thought-out risks that have the potential to benefit the whole team.
- Recognize the benefit of feedback from others, and

incorporate those ideas that can help you consistently improve.
+ Stick with long-term plans to bring goals to fruition even if they take a long time to manifest.

We create courage and clarity in our lives and in the lives of others when we have unfettered access to the positive aspects of our Wood archetype. But sometimes Wood can become unstable, stressed, and unavailable to us. Luckily, Wood gives us warning signs to help us know when this is happening.

Stressed Wood manifests as:

+ Feeling anger and frustration when limitations keep you from moving forward with your plans.
+ Not being able to maintain sustained focus on a project you once were passionate about.
+ Over-focusing on the big picture while losing sight of important details along the way.
+ Feeling less tolerant of the people around you who slow you down.
+ Not finding satisfaction in a job well done and needing to jump right into the next project to keep feeling pride.
+ Losing the clarity to make bold, quick decisions.
+ Believing winning is more important than anything else.
+ An inability to plan the next move.
+ Becoming inert and not feeling like exercising or moving as much as usual.
+ Freezing up when you hear feedback that suggests you have room to improve.

+ Not being able to stand up for yourself without feeling highly irritated.
+ Engaging in all work and no play.
+ Believing eating is only about fueling up and not for pleasure, boosting your health, or community togetherness.
+ Believing small talk is a waste of time.
+ Thinking sleep gets in the way of productivity.
+ Not seeing the benefits of meditation or calm reflection.
+ Believing speed is more important than thoroughness.
+ Feeling impatient a lot of the time.
+ Craving stimulants like caffeine to keep going.
+ Eating on the run a lot.
+ Feeling tired from working so hard.
+ Feeling like a failure if you can't keep up with the audacious pace you've set for yourself.
+ Becoming easily short-tempered.
+ Having more difficulty seeing the big picture and feeling like you're on a path to fulfilling your life's purpose.
+ Seeking bigger and bigger risks, since you're not satisfied for very long with what you have.

At its core, recognizing your strong and stressed Wood dispositions in Step One is about shifting how you use your time. Unbalanced Wood types have a tendency to rush through life hoping everything goes well and nothing gets in the way of ticking off all the items on their to-do list. In such a state, Wood types are more likely to ignore the early signs of internal stress and relationship problems. However, early detection allows us to stave off issues well before they grow into turbulent, painful situations.

Step One in the optimization process invites you to make time to notice subtle clues that may direct you to course-correct or perhaps stay right where you are and move a little faster toward your goal.

Start practicing this step by recognizing and tracking your Wood stress and strength states. Recognizing asks you to look and observe, not judge and criticize. There is no right or wrong, good or bad in these states. They're your teachers. They help you know what type of action to take so you continue to develop internal strength and expand healthy relationship skills. So just notice things like whether you openly listened to your colleague's opinion of your work or quickly reacted to argue in support of your perspective. Become aware of when you're trying to plow through challenges without evaluating them. Familiarize yourself with these lists, and remember to simply pay attention to your Wood tendencies.

Once you get used to noticing when and how your Wood states make themselves apparent in your daily life, you may also choose to track these symptoms or challenge states. Many people are pleasantly surprised at how easy it becomes to take more control over their less pleasant states and to self-regulate just by taking a moment to notice themselves throughout the day.

Over time, you may surprise yourself by spotting patterns of thoughts and behaviors you usually miss when rushing through your day. When you slow down and take the time to notice your Wood states, you may become aware that your stress thoughts and behaviors always reach a peak around certain people in your life. You may notice that when you hear critiques of your work, you jump into feelings of anger quite quickly when you never really realized you did that before. You may also start to become cognizant of the fact that when you speak up in a group, you spend more time talking about your own achievements than about those of others around you. In those moments, you may appreciate how your heightened awareness of yourself also contributes to your ability to notice the impact your thoughts, behaviors, and predilections have on other people.

Step Two:
Understanding Wood's Needs for Safety

You now know how Wood looks and feels when it's strong and when it's stressed, but let's take a look at why primary Woods get stressed out in the first place.

As Dr. Cowan teaches in the Tournesol Kids #PowerUp program—a nonprofit we created together to teach parents, teachers, and kids the skills for self-awareness, self-regulation, and empathy—we only experience our stress states when our particular needs for safety are not met. Our individual needs for feeling secure correspond directly to our primary archetype. Just as Wood's strength and stress conditions are unique, so are the particular needs a primary Wood requires to feel balanced and avoid feeling too much stress.

For example, you'll see in the list below that primary Wood people require forward movement, potential, and adventure in their lives. When Wood types go too long without these needs being met, their stressed behaviors and feelings begin manifesting. However, it's up to them to recognize which of their needs are not being met and to make a plan to bring action, challenge, and freedom back into their lives. If primary Woods were to expect others to meet their needs for challenge and speed, they would be setting themselves up for disappointment, which leads to anger and frustration toward themselves and toward the people they think "waste my time and hold me back." Ultimately, expecting others to fulfill your needs for you only drives a wedge in your relationships and stokes emotions that make it difficult for you to access your inherently trailblazing Wood strengths.

This is why I've created a "needs list" for primary Woods, inspired by what I've learned from Dr. Cowan, so you as a Trailblazer can better understand your specific needs and avoid getting stuck in destructive situations. Recognizing and meeting your individual needs for safety will help you feel strong, confident, and motivated to take good care of yourself and your relationships.

NOTE: If Wood is not your primary archetype, you can still refer to this Wood's Needs List to better understand and empathize with the primary Wood people in your life. The more skilled you become at empathizing with the needs of others, the more success you'll have in your interpersonal relationships. For more information on how to more harmoniously interact with the other Wood types in your life, turn to page 81.

WOOD'S NEEDS LIST

• Action	• Duty	• Momentum
• Activity	• Effort	• Nature
• Advancement	• Enterprise	• Objective
• Adventure	• Evolution	• Opportunity
• Ambition	• Exercise	• Option
• Assurance	• Fortitude	• Oversight
• Autonomy	• Freedom	• Participation
• Bravery	• Grit	• Plan
• Challenge	• Impact	• Possibility
• Change	• Importance	• Prestige
• Choice	• Improvement	• Progress
• Clarity	• Initiative	• Purpose
• Competition	• Intention	• Resistance
• Confidence	• Justice	• Self-confidence
• Contest	• Leadership	• Self-determination
• Debate	• Leverage	• Space
• Decision	• Liberty	• Speed
• Destination	• Logic	• Stimulation

WOOD'S NEEDS LIST (CONTINUED)

✦ Strategy	✦ Tenacity	✦ Viewpoint
✦ Struggle	✦ Tension	✦ Vision
✦ Target	✦ Truth	✦ Vitality

If your primary archetype is Wood, use the needs list to help you:

✦ Feel relief more quickly in times of challenge.
✦ Feel less critical of yourself and others.
✦ Feel more motivated to figure out how to have your
own needs met more of the time.

To help you get started, think of a current struggle you're having. Then take a look over the needs list to see if there is a need related to your struggle that you wish you could fulfill right now.

Be mindful that this needs exercise is not about what others aren't giving you or doing for you, as Dr. Cowan teaches. Instead, it's about gaining an awareness of which of your core needs for safety are not being met at that moment and figuring out what *you* can do to have them met.

Keep in mind, your individual "needs" work is about empowering yourself to observe how you're feeling and to take control over creating internal harmony. It's about figuring out how you can get your own needs met, not about expecting other people or outside circumstances to change so that you get what you want. I'd be willing to bet you've tried that before and have come up empty-handed. Expecting others to complete us simply doesn't work—sorry, Jerry McGuire!

This is not to say we shouldn't empathize with and care for each other or meet each other's needs within relationships. The sign of a strong relationship is when we can have compassion for and meet each other's shared needs for safety. Take a look back over Neha Chawla's advice for building and nurturing strong relationships on pages 36–38 for a refresher.

Remember that the only thing in this world you can control is you. Take some time to review the needs list that corresponds to your primary archetype. When your stress states creep up, pause instead of reacting. Then practice taking action to acquire the items on the list that you need in your life. Doing so will reduce the frequency and severity of your stress states and allow you to recover from them more quickly and easily. As a result, you'll feel better more of the time and enjoy more fulfilling relationships.

The highest level of having your needs met is being able to meet them for yourself. Being aware of and figuring out how to meet your needs for safety is the way to continuously grow stronger throughout your lifetime. When you are self-aware, self-reliant, empathetic, and empowered to meet your own needs, your life experience is exponentially elevated.

Step Two in the optimization process asks that you recognize which of your specific unmet Wood needs for safety are kicking up your uncomfortable emotions. The more you practice merely paying attention to your stress and strength states, the easier it will be for you to identify and even predict why you're feeling low. Making this connection subsequently brings you closer to taking control over the seemingly inexplicable ebb and flow of your emotions.

For example, a frequent stress trigger for primary Woods is feeling that someone or something is wasting their time. When primary Wood people feel they're being compelled to sublimate their agenda according to someone else's slower timetable, their fear of idleness and slowing down is provoked. In the face of this fear, a primary Wood person may feel extra body tension or become overly busy and engrossed in their work because they're trying to make up for time they think has been lost or wasted.

When left unaddressed, these irritating emotions intensify. In Wood types, this could result in:

+ Impulsive behavior
+ Hypercompetitiveness
+ Difficulty accessing enthusiasm about projects
+ Trouble staying aware of how your behavior impacts those around you

To start practicing Step Two as a primary Wood, examine a current stressor that's bothering you. Next, identify the feelings that come up for you as a result of this particular challenge. Your emotions are your need identifiers. Wood types sometimes exhibit anger in response to escalating mixed emotions. However, here I'm asking you to pause. Instead of engaging with your mixed emotions, observe them. Consider that your anger is there to help you identify your unmet needs for safety. Once you've identified all your mixed emotions, wait for a beat or two and ask yourself what unmet need(s) they're telling you that you should focus on from your needs list.

If you're feeling anxious, sad, afraid, or angry, Step Two asks you to notice it. Observe, and don't react. Try to identify what your frustrated Wood feelings are telling you that you need in that moment. Are you feeling inhibited? Are your colleagues criticizing your work too much, asking you to go back to the drawing board and reframe your plans? Are people around you engaging in too much idle chatter?

Any of these examples can dredge up uncomfortable emotions for primary Wood people, but the more you practice pausing and observing what comes up for you when you feel uncomfortable emotions, the more you'll remain calm and notice which of your needs aren't being met, instead of experiencing frustration toward others or self-critical thinking.

When you know what is causing your Wood energy to get caught up in exasperation, you grow closer to becoming resilient to your triggers on a regular basis.

Step Three:
Achieving Balance Within the Wood Archetype

Step Three in the optimization process is about taking action. This is the step for building your foundation of resilience and making new stress-response choices. This is where you begin to build new habits and behaviors, which translate into the creation of new and healthier neural pathways over time and, ultimately, balance within your primary archetype.

Armed with new information about the source of your stressors from Step Two, you're more aware of where your unpleasant feelings are coming from. You understand that they're directly related to whether or not you're having your needs for safety met. Other people and outside circumstances may initiate uncomfortable events, but how you choose to respond is ultimately your decision. If you elect to react while your Wood is unbalanced, you and those around you will spend more time in discomfort.

On the other hand, if your Wood is balanced, you will be more in control of your reactive states under stress and actually reduce the amount of time you and the others spend upset. Reducing your reactivity enables clarity of thought, creativity, smooth conflict resolution, and unconditional love. When you have more control over your stress reactions, you will live a more fulfilling and well-adjusted life.

Let's get to the core of how to achieve a balanced Wood archetype. While Wood is the power of adventure and spontaneity in relationships, if Wood is not nurtured and gently curbed to be balanced, then it can become difficult to maintain healthy and lasting connections with those you love and care for. The Wood archetype needs to support you by contributing its venturesome spirit instead of its stressed qualities. You also need your Wood to be balanced so it can help temper and balance out the stress states of the other four types within you. Ultimately, as a primary Wood, your Wood archetype needs to work for you so it can improve your life, instead of making it stressful.

Your Wood-Balancing Skills

Balanced Wood presents itself as the ability to work effectively with others to accomplish shared goals and to create opportunities and guidance that help other people realize their own desires.

As you know, Wood is forward-thinking and seeks to initiate change and advancement. But just as wood that becomes too wet or too dry or is not pruned properly cannot deliver fruit nor shade, the Wood archetype within us can become overbearing or unstable if it doesn't have a balance of what it needs. Wood's instability can manifest as becoming too preoccupied with dominating the competition or as being so attached to needing freedom that relationships feel more suffocating than rewarding.

We become balanced by taking specific and consistent action that builds and protects the body, mind, and spirit components of our archetypal nature. Eastern well-being philosophies like TCM state that whole health is not achieved by simply addressing one of these three aspects of our overall being. They teach that these aspects are inextricably connected within us. For example, a physical imbalance causes emotional unrest, which manifests as larger existential conundrums. Consummate balance is the result of a combined effort to empower all three intertwined parts. Thus, you'll notice that the tasks for balancing the Five Archetypes draw upon all three realms: mind, body, and spirit.

+ + + + +

Now that you're familiar with Steps One and Two of the optimization process, in which you learned about Wood's archetypal traits and needs for safety, it's time to learn how to balance your Wood archetype—and even how to help other Wood types do the same.

There are two important ways of doing so:

+ Self-care in the moment
+ Long-term maintenance

Wood Self-Care in the Moment

Wood self-care in a moment of heightened stress and imbalance calls for different skills from those you'll use for building resilience and ultimately balance over time.

Faced with an intense, difficult, heated situation, a primary Wood type is not going to have an easy time identifying the mixed emotions that are feeding the reactive state or coming up with creative ways to solve what likely feels like a downright attack. At the peak of a Wood type's overwhelm, they don't feel like calmly sitting down and talking through their challenges.

But in Wood's troublesome moments, such as when anger and frustration peak, Fire serves as Wood's immediate release valve. Fire activities, behaviors, thoughts, and people are the most likely to help Wood rebalance and recover from a stress trigger.

Some Fire tools for releasing the initial pressure include:

+ Identify one to three of the mixed feelings that are coming up for you in the stressful moment.
+ Assess on a scale of one to five how intense your anger is right now, one being least intense and five being most intense.
+ Practice a heart-opening yoga stretch like reverse warrior, standing goddess, or low lunge.
+ Practice a Brow, or Third-eye, Chakra yoga stretch like child's pose, dolphin pose, or sitting head to knee pose.
+ Touch or squeeze an object like a stress ball that helps you release the tension building up in the moment.

+ Look around the room and name five things you see around you that you like or that make you happy. This helps you stay in the present instead of losing yourself in a rapidly escalating frenzy about your situation.
+ Look at reminders of your successes. This could be certificates, trophies, emails, handwritten thank-you notes, photos, or diplomas.
+ Speak to a friend you can count on to be optimistic and encouraging in the face of pessimism.

If Woods are too frustrated to access Fire, they should move their bodies to blow off some steam first. Go for a run, take a brisk walk, toss a ball against a wall, or simply leave the room for a moment.

Once over the initial hurdle of emotional intensity, when a sense of calm begins to reappear, primary Woods then have easier access to skills from the other archetypes that will help expand their ability to solve the challenge that kicked up stress in the first place.

When you, as a primary Wood, feel adequately calm and prepared to begin problem solving, choose the archetype-based activities from the lists on pages 86–93 that correspond to the strengths you most need in the moment. Examples of the strengths that correspond to each type are:

+ **Wood:** You'll need to rely upon your Wood skills if your problem requires a plan, forward movement, or speed.
+ **Fire:** You'll need to draw upon your Fire skills if your problem requires optimism, deepening connections with people, or discussing your feelings.
+ **Earth:** You'll need to access your Earth skills if your issue requires collaboration with another party, teaching others a skill, or gaining an understanding of what everyone needs next to move things forward.

+ **Metal:** You'll want to dip into your Metal skills if your concern revolves around developing a new system or improving an old one, holding yourself or someone else accountable, or editing and refining a document.
+ **Water:** You'll reach for your Water skills if your issue requires more time to think things through, a deeper evaluation of all the components impacting your challenge, or sitting back and really listening to what everyone's concerns are.

Wood Long-Term Maintenance

Another way to achieve balance within your Wood archetype is to practice maintenance activities over the long term to help ensure you remain resilient in the face of stress as you progress. With a stable, reliable cache of resilience accumulated, you will more adeptly wield the skill of observing your challenges rather than reacting to them. The better you become at avoiding reactive states, the more quickly you recover from stress and return to enjoying life.

Begin your maintenance regimen by practicing activities that support your primary Wood archetype. Start by choosing one or two activities from the Wood list to practice every day.

Next, identify one or two activities from the archetype list that correspond to the archetype in which you scored the lowest. Add these items to your daily Wood archetype routine. Don't forget, it's important to practice your lowest archetype, even if it's your least favorite type of activity (which I'm willing to bet it is). Exercising your most vulnerable archetype minimizes the gap between your highest and lowest archetypes, expanding your ability to be more emotionally dexterous when challenges arise.

Finally, practice activities that correlate to the challenges you're currently facing. Here are some examples to help you identify which archetypal skills in the lists on pages 50–59 you will need and will find most helpful as a primary Wood:

+ If you find yourself reacting to criticism by believing you have failed, practice some Fire activities to remind yourself how far you've come and how amazing you are.
+ If you're feeling too reactive and stressed out by the needs of the people around you, focus on expanding your Earth skills to build more tolerance and appreciation for the contributions of others.
+ If you find yourself feeling run-down because you're over-focusing on driving projects forward, it's time to exercise your Metal skills and structure some time for self-care into your routine.
+ If you always feel like you're in a rush and are having a hard time focusing your mind for solving complex problems, empower your ability to reflect and find calm with some Water abilities.

Choose from among these Wood activities to get you started on building your Wood maintenance regimen:

+ Observe and track the times you experience restlessness or impatience in response to people or activities you believe move too slowly. Pay attention to these instances and rank on a scale of 1 to 10 how much anger you feel as a result. Simply track it. This exercise will help you build resilience to these situations in the long run.
+ Ask your spouse or someone you live with to give you a gentle signal if they notice you starting to become

agitated. Sometimes those around us notice our Wood frustration sooner than we notice it ourselves, and their mild signal can help keep our anger from escalating.

- Pay attention to the times you feel compelled to win for the sake of winning. Just observe; don't judge yourself for it.
- Practice making backup plans for what you'll do if your first ideas don't produce the outcome you had hoped. Planning ahead for possible hiccups makes you a better leader and helps you avoid the frustration of feeling your ideas didn't work.
- Exercise each day, but try not to overdo it all the time. Consider working in some slower, more precise exercises that require balancing breath with moving and stretching, like yoga, tai chi, or qi gong.
- Spend time outside in nature.
- Find something you can be in charge of, win, or lead. This could be coaching a team, leading a committee for a nonprofit or a house of worship, or heading up a company or division at work. Start a business, invent a modernized technique, or train for a competitive sport like a marathon or a triathlon.
- Work in a vocation or field that gives you the opportunity to direct something, to make decisions and initiate action that moves projects forward.
- Make life plans—short-term and long-term—so you can look back and measure how far you've come toward achieving your dreams and aspirations.
- Surround yourself with soothing colors, like green, dark blue, and indigo.
- Plant a garden, or add some houseplants to your home or office.

+ Remind yourself of your accomplishments and how far you've come toward reaching your goals for works that are still in progress.
+ Plan regular adventures, outings, or vacations.
+ Regularly schedule a massage.

Water-Building Activities

+ Make sure you're drinking enough water each day.
+ Build in time each day to slow down, whether it's journaling, reading, watching a movie, or getting a manicure. Allow your body and mind some time to recover from the hard work they do each day to keep up your vitality.
+ Listen to gentle, calming music.
+ Read a book you enjoy.
+ Start a meditation practice. Take note of how regular meditation will help you achieve more, and achieve it faster. Make sure it's a practice that feels like a fit for you; Wood people tend to become restless and don't always see the benefit in slowing down.
+ Take baths with lavender oil or another scent that makes you feel calm.
+ Swim.
+ Take a slow walk in nature, preferably near a body of water.
+ Try to get to bed before midnight—preferably as close to 10:00 p.m. as possible.
+ Massage your hands and feet before bed; coconut oil is a good choice, and it's safe and readily available.
+ Rest quietly for a few minutes each day with one hand held over your heart and the other over your abdomen.

+ Think of past times when you've felt obstacles were keeping you from moving forward, but in the end you prevailed.

Fire-Building Activities

+ Build and nurture friendships with optimistic, trustworthy, communicative, emotionally balanced people, and ask them to subtly convey to you times when they notice you're in the early stages of agitation. Wood tends to move quickly into heightened states of irritability, so a good friend who helps you notice the initial moments can help you become more aware of your anger before it gets too intense.
+ Have fun! Build in time to kick back with friends and enjoy fun activities together.
+ Practice noticing and articulating your feelings. Start by recognizing and saying how you feel—first to yourself; then, as you feel more comfortable with this practice, share your feelings with important people in your life. See if you can start to identify the mixed and more complex emotions that come up. Wood feels frustration and anger quickly, but there are a variety of emotions underneath. See how many you can identify. Over time, you won't feel as though this is a waste of time. You'll begin to notice that it helps you move through feelings of anger more quickly and sometimes even avoid those angry feelings altogether.
+ Every day, smile at yourself in the mirror and at other people; a smile spreads joy and is said to reduce cortisol production.

+ Practice regular heart-opening and third-eye yoga stretches as listed above on page 83 in the Wood Self-Care in the Moment section.
+ Watch entertaining or inspirational speakers on video or in person.
+ Consider joining a laughter yoga class or an improvisational/stand-up comedy class, where you can practice humor and practice receiving constructive feedback on your performance.

Earth-Building Activities

+ Become part of a community or group. This could be a sports team, a religious or spiritual group, a non-profit board, a group of parents, or perhaps a social justice community. Choose something that you feel passionate about and want to contribute to.
+ Mentor someone whose life you could help advance.
+ Make sure you're setting aside time to eat peacefully, sitting down and appreciating your meals. Wood tends to eat on the run.
+ Dedicate a moment to pause and pay attention to the relationship your body has with your food. Notice whether you feel constipated, gassy, or bloated, or have acid reflux. If your digestion feels shaky, seek the guidance of a nutrition specialist to get it back on track.
+ Find one item or meal to eat mindfully each day, appreciating every bite, chewing slowly, and pausing between bites. Consider trying to chew twenty times per bite.
+ Close your eyes and bring your awareness to your body. Can you identify where your current stress sits

in your body? Focus your awareness on that spot, breathe into it, and exhale with strength through your mouth. During your exhale, imagine the breath is leaving your body through the spot where you envisioned your stress lingering.

+ Practice asking others how they're doing for the sole purpose of building a connection and showing you really care about them. Engage in pleasantries like this a few times a week, and see if you can remember details about the other person. Refer back to those details the next time you see them to start building compassionate bonds. Details could include birthdays, what their kids are up to, recent vacations, or educational pursuits.

+ Practice identifying what someone you care about needs once per day. After you've done this activity for a while, consider answering the needs you've identified in the people you've observed. This could be anything from spending a few minutes listening to someone's problems to offering help with running errands or giving advice on how to start an exercise routine.

+ Stick to one or two cups of coffee per day, or add a quarter teaspoon of cardamom powder to your coffee to reduce the potentially jittery effect of the caffeine.

+ Don't rely too much on alcohol to calm you or help you slow down.

Metal-Building Activities

+ Create some structure within your day, and do your best to stick to it—whether it's a morning routine; eating meals around the same time each day; creating a bedtime routine or a routine for prayer or worship; taking up a hobby and attending classes or practicing newly acquired skills regularly; or keeping a calendar of your activities and following it.
+ Come up with a system for how to measure your success in adhering to your routines.
+ Adopt a breathwork practice that you like and do it regularly.
+ Upon waking and right before you fall asleep at night, think of one to three people for whom you're grateful.
+ Participate in self-care that gives you personalized attention, like acupuncture or Ayurveda.
+ Use aromatherapy at home and at work, if appropriate. Aromas that support balanced Wood include:

+ Angelica seed	+ Jasmine	+ Sandalwood
+ Lavender	+ Lemon	+ Clary sage
+ Hyacinth	+ Rosemary	+ Cedar wood
+ Camphor	+ Frankincense	+ Cypress
+ Eucalyptus	+ Blue chamomile	

+ Choose or create your own ritual that means something to you, and practice it regularly.
+ Establish a dedicated space in your home for a quiet moment of reflection and appreciation each day. This could be a shelf or small table with a candle, photos

of people you love, or mementos of times and places that hold meaning.

+ Practice something that requires coordination and focus to accelerate your talent, like playing a musical instrument or creating a painting or sculpture.

+ Look around the room and name five things you see. This helps you appreciate and stay in the present instead of getting frustrated about not moving fast enough out of your current dilemma.

+ Build in time for a gratitude practice, thinking of people and things in your life for which you're grateful and listing reasons why.

Ultimately, your Wood archetype is balanced when you:

+ Are led more by foresight and thoughtful intention than unpredictable arousal.

+ Have more control over the speed at which you pursue and complete projects, tasks, and ideas.

+ Notice when you start to feel emotions of anger before they get heightened.

+ Get good sleep.

+ Include self-care as part of your regular regimen.

+ Set aside time to eat meals calmly and meditatively as often as you can.

+ Find satisfaction in coaching others to become successful in reaching their goals.

+ Take constructive feedback as an opportunity to grow and learn something new for yourself instead of receiving it as criticism you feel you must rebut.

+ Sometimes play games just for the fun of it and

to build comradery, without the need to win every
game.

+ Have an easier time recognizing when you need help,
and be open to asking for it.

+ Round out your life with some consistent healthy lifestyle engagement, like establishing a regular mealtime,
eating sitting down instead of on the run, meditating,
journaling, taking up a religious or spiritual practice,
or volunteering.

+ Feel like you can balance all the responsibilities on
your plate better.

+ Feel fulfilled and passionate about your work, not frequently antsy because you need a change.

+ Catch yourself before irritable feelings become outbursts.

+ Become more aware of the feelings and needs of the
other people in the room.

+ Stay on schedule more often.

+ Are able to take responsibility for your own actions
and decisions, even when things don't go well.

+ Consistently move forward despite complications and
snags along the way.

+ Work on behalf of all people to bring them justice
and fairness, especially in the face of discrimination
and inequity.

+ Are aware of your strength and stress states.

+ Know your needs for safety.

+ Are able to predict triggers and recover with ease in
times of stress more of the time.

Harmonization

I don't want to leave you hanging, wondering when and how you'll know that you're in harmony as a primary Wood.

Again, harmonization is not an absence of stress and challenge. For primary Woods, it's about being able to navigate the challenging moments in your own life while empathizing with and supporting those around you whose Wood archetype may be low and in need of a boost. At its core, harmonization allows you to have unconditional love for yourself and those around you.

When you, as a primary Wood, are harmonized, you're likely to experience many, if not all, of the attitudes and behaviors noted below.

+ You consistently notice, honor, and take control over the connections
    + between the exercise you get and how much stress you feel.
    + between how in tune you are with your emotions and how quickly you escalate into states of anger.
    + between the food you eat/the strength of your digestion and how you feel emotionally.
    + between the amount of time you spend slowing down and staying organized and the quality of your work.
    + between the sleep you get and how thoroughly you examine all sides of a potential project.
+ You cherish spending time alone resting, retreating, and reflecting.
+ You have the drive to consistently follow through on and complete initiatives.
+ You care deeply for people who want to sit and spend time getting to know you.

+ You enjoy coaching people more.
+ You stand up for others more.
+ Your exercise is balanced, and you don't get easily injured when you work out.
+ You applaud other people's ideas and suggestions and believe they're worth implementing.

WOOD IN RELATIONSHIPS

As our personal awareness and resilience in the face of stress expands, we are less triggered by other people's opinions, moods, and tendencies. We also become less likely to attach to relationships that don't serve us well or in which our needs for safety aren't being met. As we strengthen our individual Five Archetypes skills, we are better equipped to form equally strong bonds with individuals from any one of the Five Archetypes because we see the benefit and the beauty of the gifts they each bring to the companionship.

In this section, primary Woods will gain guidance for building and maintaining propitious relationships, and non-primary Woods will learn how to engage in healthy relationships with primary Wood types.

If You Are a Wood/Trailblazer

To be a good Wood partner in any relationship, practice staying in balance by knowing your strengths, challenges, and needs, and by practicing the Wood long-term maintenance activities starting on page 86 to remain a consistently stable partner. This will ensure you approach relationship challenges from a place of calm compassion for yourself and your companions.

When you commit to doing the work that keeps your Wood in balance, you contribute the following strengths to your interpersonal relationships:

+ Seeking out and providing opportunities for joint adventure and growth.
+ Encouraging partners not to give up, but to plow ahead through adversity.
+ Helping others to not get stuck on the small details and instead see the bigger picture.
+ Standing up for your partners or kids in the face of injustice.
+ Envisioning a bold future and creating a plan for you both to get there.
+ Awakening others to new and better possibilities together.
+ Not being afraid of tension in a relationship, but rather seeing it as an opportunity for growth and promising new potential.
+ Being reliable and sticking with healthy relationships, even when things get hard.
+ Taking the reins in times of conflict to make sure you don't both get mired in minutia and worries instead of moving toward a better future.
+ Believing there's no obstacle unsurmountable in the relationship.
+ Protecting the tribe or the family with every ounce of your being.
+ Being spontaneous and prepared for a challenge or an adventure at the drop of a hat.
+ Empowering partners to realize their own dreams.

When your Wood is balanced, you also possess the following characteristics that benefit the global community:

- You are benevolent and just, determined to change the world for the better.
- You stand up for the less fortunate and lead the march for justice.
- You instigate movements for people's rights and ensure the process unfolds swiftly and adroitly.
- You forcefully push forward with a righteous agenda, and don't shrink back in the face of hurdles and outdated ways of doing things.
- You have no fear of unchartered territory.
- You implement deft plans, mapping the way ahead for all to follow.
- You transform antiquated systems that no longer serve humanity.
- You don't crumble under the pressure of conflicting opinions and deadlines.
- You seek solutions when others start to worry there's no possible way forward.
- You won't give up on the cause.
- You refuse to waste time on activities that don't support the end goal.

On the other hand, when your primary Wood is not in balance, it shows up in your interpersonal relationships as:

- Becoming tense when someone disagrees with your opinion.
- Believing other people are too critical of you.

+ Seeing other people's input as constricting your ability to move a task forward.
+ Overreacting and becoming unnerved when your partner says no.
+ Not wanting to be in a relationship because it feels too confining.
+ Not wanting to conform to your partner's relationship "rules."
+ Feeling that it's "my way or the highway."
+ Not seeing the value in listening to other people's opinions.
+ Thinking that needing someone else is the same as being weak.
+ Becoming too competitive with your partner and not seeing the benefit of fighting for the same goals.
+ Blaming others for things that don't go as planned.
+ Being unwilling to wait for your partner to catch up because their slowness is holding you back.
+ Requiring your partner to respond quickly to your instructions.
+ Working so many hours that there's no time to nurture a relationship.
+ Becoming less aware of the emotional impact your reactionary and stress states have on others.
+ Becoming easily aggravated when your partner tells you what to do.
+ Having difficulty staying in one job or relationship for very long.

When your primary Wood is unbalanced, watch out for these potential behaviors that could manifest and affect your global community:

+ Losing sight of the greater good and only fighting to further your own individual goals.
+ Not taking adequate time to make sure your resolutions are designed well enough to be sustainable for the long haul.
+ Pushing staff and team members too hard, not recognizing small advances and contributions.
+ Breaking rules that are in place for important reasons solely to get things done on your own time frame.
+ Being so eager to move full speed ahead that you become immune to others' feelings along the way.
+ Directing the team to do it your way even before examining all possible routes recommended by others.
+ Having ideas for making the world a better place that veer more toward impulsive and aggressive than compassionately inclusive, heroic, and brave.

If You Have a Relationship with a Wood/Trailblazer

In the following pages, you will learn how primary Woods exhibit themselves at work, in intimate relationships, and as parents. Remember, *The Five Archetypes* is a primer for beginners, so I'm just touching on the basic concepts to help you understand, evaluate, and adjust the flow of the primary Wood archetype within you for the best personal and interpersonal outcomes.

The Wood Employee or Coworker

When applied to the workplace, the Five Archetypes method expands your ability and the ability of your coworkers to get things done efficiently. Moreover, when employees and colleagues feel safe, seen, understood, and appreciated in the workplace, they navigate challenges more easily and therefore are less reactive when in stress states, which ultimately translates to a healthier bottom line.

To enhance your awareness of times when your Wood staff or co-workers feel safe and when they feel insecure, there are some common tendencies to watch out for. When you see your colleagues exhibiting their insecure states, it's time to pause and fortify yourself so you don't jump into your reactive states as a result. Get to know these common strengths, needs, and stress states:

+ Strengths at Work: A Wood employee clearly envisions the path ahead and takes decisive action to make sure the company meets goals.
+ Needs at Work: Woods like to be challenged and work well under pressure. They like action, speed, and competitiveness.
+ Potential Challenges and Stress States: When stressed, Woods tend to perceive others' ideas and criticisms as attacks. These perceptions can lead to feelings of anger and frustration. A stressed primary Wood may also focus too much on getting projects done quickly and overlook small yet significant details for creating a meticulously designed product.
+ Here's how to nurture Wood employees over time and how to help them release stress in the moment.
    + Support in the Moment: Hope and optimism help Woods reduce reactionary states in the moment. Get specific, acknowledging their terrific ideas and the value their drive and grit contribute to the company. Be positive with your frustrated Wood employees or coworkers. Over time, encourage them to regularly express their varied and mixed feelings about challenges and difficult interactions.

This will help them know how to access more complex emotions and avoid overreacting in times of emotional turbulence.

+ Ongoing Encouragement: If you manage Woods in the workplace, reinforce the importance of regular breaks for rest and reflecting on open projects and relationships. Emphasize the significance of slowing down to evaluate the less obvious components of a successful pitch or project. Consider scheduling regular time in the calendar for these reflective conversations with a nod toward how these meetings improve the organization's success rate, which will ultimately be highly motivating for a Wood employee.

The Wood Friend

Enjoying mutually gratifying friendships starts with *you* knowing how to be a good friend to others. To consistently show up as a steady, sincere, reliable friend, check out these Five Archetypes guidelines:

+ Learn your primary archetype strengths, challenges, and needs so you can practice becoming and staying self-aware.
+ Make sure your needs for safety are being met within the relationship.
+ Recognize and take responsibility for your reactive states and practice your self-regulation techniques.
+ Adopt a mind-set in which you see challenge as an invitation to grow, not an excuse to judge or criticize others.
+ Discover your friends' needs for safety so you can practice compassionate consideration.

How Do We Nurture Lasting Friendships?

As a friendship grows, how do we continue to nurture the bond using the Five Archetypes method? When you know your friend's primary archetype, you will better understand what makes them feel safe and what makes them feel insecure. Here are some additional suggestions for what primary Wood people will likely appreciate in a close friendship.

Wood likes spending time with people who:

+ Are always up for a challenge or adventure.
+ Enjoy a good debate.
+ Let them make the plans a lot of the time.
+ Like to be active and engage in sports or spend time outdoors.

Helping a Wood Friend in Stress

When you care about someone, you sympathize with their pain and want them to feel better. The Five Archetypes method helps us understand that people have unique stress triggers and also have different paths to de-stressing. Here's how to help your primary Wood friends recover more quickly from stress states.

Uplift a Wood friend by praising his ideas. Share how excited you are about what he's devised and envisioned as the way forward. Your Wood friend will also benefit from physically getting away from the stressful situation, taking a walk outside, or getting a drink of water.

The Wood Romantic Partner

Primary Wood people keep things moving in a relationship. They get you outside hiking, biking, running, exploring. On Sunday morning, they'll have you up early for an activity. No lying around in bed for your Wood partner, although at bedtime, he may fall asleep quickly, having been so active all day.

Your Wood partner will also stand up for your rights, protecting you with vigilance from anyone who attempts to knock you down. He has big plans for your future and makes sure you reach those goals together in strength.

When Woods feel insecure, they exhibit specific patterns of disharmony in a relationship. Stressed Woods fear feeling trapped in a relationship with no way out and may desire freedom over the confinement of the union. When they're not feeling strong, they have the potential to become pushy and argumentative without the ability to pause and notice what their partner feels or needs.

Here are some tips for how you can be a strong partner to a primary Wood type:

- ◆ Do: Give him a choice of which path to take. He likes to feel in control of his destiny.
- ◆ Don't: Insist on winning every backgammon game, even if you're better. Let him win once in a while. It'll make him feel good.
- ◆ Help Them Refocus in Stress: Boost their sense of self-confidence by telling them how much you admire their ideas and accomplishments.
- ◆ Best Form of Consistent Encouragement: Build in quiet time to your week with your Wood partner. He is always on the go, and adequate rest will empower him with enough strength to stay energized.

The Parent–Wood Child Relationship

Your parent-child relationship is impacted not only by the intersection between your and your child's primary archetypes but also by how you perceive your purpose as a parent. When you see your parental role as compassionate guide and teacher and empower your kids to master life skills so they become strong, resilient adults, you're more likely to build a strong relationship with your child and feel fulfilled by the parenting journey.

To create a gratifying and lasting relationship with your primary Wood child using the Five Archetypes method, start by identifying and balancing your own primary archetype. Get to know yourself in strength and in stress. Understand your button pushers so that you're best able to remain in a state of resilience and compassionate power when faced with your triggers. You'll be the most outstanding advocate for and will nurture a respectful, strong relationship with your child when you serve as a heroic example of how to manage stress, triggers, and disappointment.

Then find out your child's primary archetype. Help him become more self-aware and self-reliant by teaching him how to recognize and celebrate his gifts. Empower him to overcome his stress states with ease by understanding what pushes his buttons and giving him the Five Archetypes tools to become more resilient to his triggers.

Dr. Cowan is a pioneer of using the five types as a methodology for healthy child development. Here are some points, inspired by his work, to keep in mind when parenting a child whose primary archetype is Wood:

+ Learning style: Wood kids learn by doing, trying, exploring. They're not afraid to risk skinned knees and bruised elbows.
+ Sleeping: Wood kids like to be on the move, so be prepared for early risers.
+ Eating: Wood kids may prefer to eat on the run. Encourage them to stay at the table with the family by asking them to tell you about their plans, achievements, and wins.

+ Exercise: Encourage Wood kids' love of exercise and teach them about healthy competition. Help them to become team players and to learn that there is value in helping everyone succeed, not just in self-advancement.

+ Feelings: When Wood kids are not at their best, they tend to jump quickly into anger. It's important to help your Wood kids learn about gradations of anger and to pay attention to the subtle clues and changes in their feelings in response to internal and external circumstances. This way your Wood kids will learn to have more control over their reactions to disappointment.

WOOD AYURVEDIC PRACTICES

Wood people participate in wellness activities that reinforce a sense of accomplishment and competitiveness. They're more likely to maintain an exercise routine and thrive when they can see and measure their progress in comparison to others, or can appreciate how they've improved their speed, muscle mass, or stamina. The kinds of fitness activities Wood people enjoy include bodybuilding, competitive sports, training for marathons, and participating in challenging obstacle races.

Primary Wood types will also benefit from regular meditation, but they may find it difficult to dedicate regular time to this practice. A common Wood pitfall is rushing ahead without pausing and failing to pay attention to the more subtle aspects of an issue. Devoting time to a meditation practice helps protect them from taking hasty action in other areas of their lives. Woods may also be more inclined to stick to a meditation practice if they can directly link the practice to improving their performance. There's a lot of research that supports this phenomenon, so Wood people: Check it out! If you focus your wellness pursuits around competition and personal improvement, you will more likely be pleased with the program.

With regard to incorporating Ayurvedic wellness practices into your everyday life, remember that the Wood archetype corresponds to the sixth Chakra. In the chart on the next page, you will find some gentle Ayurvedic practices that will help engage and balance this chakra.

The sixth Chakra is known as the Brow, or Third Eye, Chakra. According to Ayurveda, the Brow Chakra governs clear vision that transcends time and space; when in balance, it correlates to the Wood archetype's ability to see the path ahead for themselves and others without being impacted by irritating emotions and perceived obstacles.

Using Ayurvedic practices is a safe and empowering option to complement any health-care regimen. Peruse the selection of Ayurvedic lifestyle practices below that correspond to your primary Wood archetype. Try the ones that feel like a good fit as you assemble your menu of healthy lifestyle practices.

Sixth Chakra—Brow or Third Eye

Oversees: Wisdom, clarity, moving from logical mind to intuitive mind, insight, visualization, fantasy
Location: Pituitary gland, pineal gland, skull, senses, left eye, cerebellum, nose, central nervous system, autonomic nervous system
Colors: Dark blue, indigo
Mantra: Om
Yoga: Child's pose, half-standing forward bend, warrior three, revolved lunge pose, locust pose, camel pose
Gemstones: Amethyst, labradorite, moldavite, lapis lazuli, amazonite
Mudra (a hand gesture that's said to stimulate a specific sense of focus and balance): Shuni mudra, ahamkara mudra
Foot marma (a pressure point that's said to enhance mind-body balance when massaged): Halfway down the outside edge of the pinky toe
Aromatherapy: Angelica seed, lavender, hyacinth, camphor, eucalyptus, jasmine, lemon, rosemary, frankincense, blue chamomile, sandalwood, clary sage, cedar wood, cypress
Taste: Pungent

A Final Note to Primary Woods

Dear Wood Friends,

A few words of encouragement as you venture out with a Five Archetypes perspective on life:

Remember, your need for speed can actually hold you back from achieving goals and moving on to the next cool project if that need isn't balanced with skills and behaviors from the other four archetypes. Experiment with what it's like to take your time, pause, and notice subtle details you previously overlooked, and pace yourself. You may be pleasantly surprised at how much more you achieve.

You are unparalleled in your ability to stick with ventures and make them happen. I am indebted to you for:

- *Always fueling my Fire so I believe in myself.*
- *Pushing me to follow my dreams so I don't get mired in self-doubt.*
- *Reminding me to exercise because it's good for me even when it's not all that fun.*

I wrote a haiku for you in honor of the gifts you bestow upon the world.

> *Your green shoots burst forth*
> *Not one rock obscures your path*
> *You are beloved*

With appreciation and humility,
Carey

FIRE

THE OPTIMIST

I f you scored highest in Fire traits on your assessment and have confirmed that your results are accurate, then Fire is considered your primary archetype.

When Fire is your primary archetype, its incandescence directs the way you interact with your environment. You share the gifts of joy, optimism, possibility, and vivacity with the world.

Fire is the dancing energy inside you that craves fun, excitement, entertainment, romance, and intimacy. It's the natural inclination to make and sustain eye contact, even and especially with people you don't know yet. Fire is the exuberant desire to eat dessert first and stay up all night partying. It's the silliness ignited when you're out with your favorite childhood friends, behaving with whimsy and mischievousness, impervious to boundaries and social mores.

Fire is ruled by the heart and is the voice inside that shouts from the rooftops, "Focus on the bright side, baby!" Fire is the delightful sparkle in your eye that gleams at the prospect of inspiring positive change in someone who needs that extra bit of encouragement. It's what you tap into when you identify so deeply with someone else's feelings that you cry or laugh along with them. Fire is the openness to trust your gut and take a risk on affiliating with a new person or idea before having done your due diligence.

Considered the "cheerful entertainer" in friendships, primary Fire types remind you to feel hopeful and help you feel connected to your own glorious emotions. Seeing you happy is incredibly satisfying to them and reassures their own sense of self-worth.

The Fire archetype, also known as "The Optimist," is associated with affection, wonder, and delight. When Fire is your primary archetype, these attributes comprise your essence. On the flip side, Fire's typical lifestyle challenges revolve around preventing burnout and overcoming the fear of losing love.

If Fire is not your primary archetype, you will still have some amount of Fire in your nature, so in order to achieve and maintain harmony throughout your lifetime, it's essential that you know where your Fire ranks with respect to the other four archetypes and that you practice the skills that help keep the Fire in your nature strong. The long-term maintenance practices beginning on page 132 will help you both optimize your primary Fire and harmonize, as well as build a firm foundation of resilience in the face of stress and empathy toward yourself and others. If Fire is your primary, practicing your long-term maintenance activities will naturally reduce the frequency and intensity of the panic or anxiety you experience when you're feeling unsafe. If Fire is your lowest, practicing these activities will increase your emotional flexibility and spur you to feel more optimistic about the potential for advantageous and positive outcomes.

When Fire Is Your Primary Archetype

If Fire is your primary or is tied as one of your two primaries, then this chapter applies most directly to you and how you understand and empower yourself and your relationships.

As a primary Fire, you tend to go through life wearing those proverbial rose-colored glasses. You have unfettered access to the most powerful of the Fire behaviors. When you're feeling on top of the world, the essence of the Fire archetype precedes you when you walk into a room. On the other end of the spectrum, insecure Fire thoughts and behaviors rule the way you experience and engage with stress.

Primary Fire types live their highest spiritual purpose through inspiring joy in others and creating a safe environment in which others can freely and openly express their emotions. With a glass-half-full outlook, Fire will always remind you that things will surely improve. Fire types endeavor to ensure that others feel happy and upbeat as well—never forlorn or hopeless. Fire is driven to teach that getting stuck in the mire of negativity will drag you down and make it hard to live your best life. Fires hope that as a result of these efforts, others will begin to model positivity even in the face of disappointment, fear, and worry.

Fires who feel grounded, self-aware, and secure in who they are will embody distinct traits in their physical, mental, and spiritual being. Physically, Fire types delight in fun, frolic, relaxing, and playing. Mentally, Fire types maintain a strong sense of emotional awareness, flexibility, and balance. Spiritually, Fire types embody and share the gift of joy even when sad things happen that are out of their control.

When your primary archetype is Fire, you'll also exhibit specific inherent capabilities and attitudes. These patterns persist and are expressed in your personal behaviors, the self-care activities you favor, and the way others perceive you.

Here are a couple of basic Fire archetype indicators to be aware of: When feeling resilient, a primary Fire person serves as a source of optimism and hope for their own life trajectory and for that of those around them. On the other hand, when feeling insecure, the Fire type becomes oversensitive and tends toward panic and anxiety.

Chronic anxiety is known to have significant health implications on the body over time. This is why it's important for Fires to recognize when it's time to self-regulate, rather than react in a maladaptive manner when faced with challenge. Sometimes we become so caught up in our dysfunctional thoughts and belief patterns that we can't easily distinguish between what we believe to be rightful action and what is actually panicky, reactive behavior. To help you know when you're in a state of imbalance and are more likely to make a dysfunctional choice, Fire types should be on the lookout for times when they:

+ Become too idealistic about potential projects before doing their due diligence.
+ Care too much about people not paying attention to them.
+ Overly skew behavior toward what is pleasing or fun instead of tending to necessary tasks.

The ultimate outcomes I hope you achieve as a result of practicing the Five Archetypes method as a primary Fire are twofold: self-empowerment and empathy for others. I want you to strengthen your personal resolve. I want you to know your unique brand of Fire-centered resilience so you can exercise it in the face of friction and conflict. When life's influences and forces lead you toward choices and behaviors that feel most Fire-type comfortable, like worrying more about people liking you than about ending harmful relationships, I want you to have the awareness to pause and recognize that your comfort zone is not always your sacred path. With time and patience, you will establish a foundation of insight and understanding for how to maintain your individuality while simultaneously enveloping those around you with compassion and kindness.

When Fire Is Your Secondary Archetype

If Fire is your secondary archetype, it modifies your primary way of engaging in the world, meaning Fire behaviors and proclivities more often reveal themselves within your character than your lower three archetypal traits, but not as much as your primary traits.

For instance, as a secondary Fire, you may notice that Fire-specific challenges, such as being ignored or not included, hurt your feelings some of the time. While Fire won't be the knee-jerk way you react when you're most agitated, you will notice times when you have Fire needs and feel Fire aggravations. Arm yourself with the Fire knowledge in this chapter so you have access to Fire-balancing activities when the need arises.

Take a look at some archetype-based traits you may notice in yourself or others who are secondary Fires:

+ Wood people with secondary Fire will delight in a healthy debate with you, but will want to make sure you still like them at the end of the conversation.
+ Earth people with secondary Fire will teach you new skills and tell you wonderful stories, and they'll care a lot about whether you're having fun during the conversation.
+ Metal people with secondary Fire have high standards, but are more emotionally flexible and less critical of people who don't share the same values.
+ Water people with secondary Fire crave alone time, but balance out solitude with a healthy dose of relaxed socializing.

When Fire Is Your Lowest Archetype

Knowing that Fire is your lowest archetype sheds light on the archetype-based skills that may be harder for you to access overall. The scarcity of Fire will also be more obvious to you in times of stress, when you feel uncomfortable in social situations, or when you're too stuck on the negatives.

If Fire is your lowest archetype, it may be challenging for you to identify with your own or other people's feelings. You may judge or criticize certain feelings as something you or others shouldn't have. You may also have a more difficult time recovering from life's big and small struggles and get stuck on the details of a problem rather than letting them go. Additionally, people who score lowest in Fire may also struggle to find ways to uplift someone who's struggling; their "Pollyanna" muscle is the one in most need of flexing. Those who score lowest in the Fire archetype may also find that they believe focusing on emotions or engaging in too much playfulness can be a waste of time.

Having an awareness of your lowest archetype, however, can show you where you need to focus your energy so you can start building overall resilience to daily stress. Recognizing that Fire is your lowest archetype and doing the work to increase your Fire traits will propel you to build more rewarding interpersonal relationships, improve your ability to share how you feel, and become more comfortable being intimate.

✦ ✦ ✦ ✦ ✦

We're just starting out on our journey together employing the Five Archetypes in our life-success strategy. While you may notice nuances within your scores that give rise to questions, in this primer we're focusing on offering a basis for understanding the overarching concepts, along with some of the most helpful day-to-day knowledge for self-improvement.

THE FIVE ARCHETYPES METHOD

Optimization

The Five Archetypes method begins with optimization, a process that comprises three steps, which remain the same no matter which archetype is your primary. They are:

1. Recognize your primary archetype's strength and stress states.
2. Understand your primary archetype's individual needs for safety.
3. Achieve balance within your primary archetype.

As a result of optimizing your primary archetype, you will cultivate more empathy and compassion—for yourself and others—and replace old, ineffectual patterns with empowerment. You will embody stability and security in the face of upset. Optimization will also give you elegance and agility at times when you're feeling powerless or tossed about like a rudderless sailboat in response to unpredictable and unstable predicaments—and help you navigate those unchartered waters with more grace and stability.

Step One:
Recognizing Fire's Strength and Stress States

When your Fire archetype is balanced, you will notice that it contributes the strengths of joy, optimism, possibility, and effervescence to your life, to your relationships, and to the broader community.

A balanced Fire also helps us:

+ Heal from grief.
+ Think of creative, outside-the-box solutions.
+ Show compassion.
+ Fall in love.
+ Connect with our feelings.
+ Initiate new possibilities.
+ Create variety in otherwise monotonous tasks and circumstances.
+ Believe in the potential of positive change.
+ Make new friends.
+ Tap into and trust our gut or intuition.
+ Realize that uncomfortable feelings are eventually going to pass.
+ Laugh out loud.
+ Thoroughly savor the taste of food you love, luxuriating in every morsel.
+ Encourage people to believe in themselves.
+ Make even the most boring and mundane experiences fun.
+ Entertain others at parties.
+ Find true joy in all experiences, whether they're difficult or fun.
+ Tell people how remarkable their ideas and accomplishments are.
+ Remind people that everything really is going to end up all right.
+ Electrify an audience with our zeal.
+ Have hope that people who are stuck feeling sad will recover and feel better quickly.
+ Feel excitement for what is next.
+ Get silly.

+ Tell jokes.
+ Feel passionate about projects, hobbies, and work interests.
+ Look forward to making new friends.
+ Enjoy making eye contact and sharing smiles.
+ Take pleasure in balancing several different projects at once.
+ Relish intimate conversations.

We live more delightful lives when we have unfettered access to the positive aspects of our Fire. But sometimes, such as when we're feeling stressed or uneasy, our Fire becomes unstable and is not as available to us. When this happens, we don't feel joyous or connected, and it's difficult to focus on the bright side. Luckily, Fire gives us warning signs to help us know when our stress states are getting the better of us and we need to take a step back and rebalance.

Stressed Fire manifests as:

+ Having difficulty sleeping.
+ Not being able to remember details.
+ Being too easily distractible.
+ Experiencing feelings of anxiety or panic.
+ Being unable to focus.
+ Feeling restless.
+ Being unable to access inspiration.
+ Feeling powerless to tap into your own sense of greater purpose.
+ Being disorganized.
+ Being too gullible.
+ Having trouble staying present in a conversation.
+ Experiencing exaggerated mood swings.

+ Feeling burnout and exhaustion.
+ Very easily becoming overly sad.
+ Being aloof and indifferent.
+ Being excessively enthusiastic.
+ Not being able to practice or do the same thing over and over.
+ Having difficulty seeing the bright side.
+ Aching to recover so quickly from challenges that you avoid taking the time to learn from mistakes.
+ Being impatient while waiting for discomfort to abate.
+ Needing happy emotions to return very quickly.
+ Having instant and intense emotional reactions to little things.
+ Getting too excited about potential.
+ Saying yes to too many things.

At its core, recognizing your strong and stressed Fire characteristics in Step One is about shifting how you use your time. Many of us rush through life, hoping everything goes well and nothing gets in the way of our ticking off all the items on our to-do list. In such a state, we are more likely to ignore the early signs of internal stress and relationship problems. However, early detection allows us to stave off issues well before they become gnarly, painful situations.

Step One in the optimization process invites you to make time to notice subtle clues that may direct you to course-correct, or perhaps stay right where you are and move a little faster toward your goal.

Start practicing this step by recognizing and tracking your Fire stress and strength states. Recognizing asks you to look and observe, not judge and criticize. There is no right or wrong, good or bad in these states. They're your teachers. They help you know what type of action to take so you continue to develop internal strength and expand healthy relationship skills. So notice whether or not you chose to make eye contact and smile at someone and how you felt about whether or not they reciprocated. Become aware of times when you're trying to avoid sad feelings. Familiarize yourself with these things, and remember to simply pay attention to your Fire.

Once you get used to noticing when and how your Fire states make themselves apparent in your daily life, you may also choose to track symptoms or challenge states. Many people are pleasantly surprised at how easy it becomes to take more control over their less pleasant states and return to balance just by taking a little time to track these tendencies throughout the day.

Over time, you may surprise yourself by noticing patterns of thoughts and behaviors you usually miss when simply rushing from one moment to the next. When you slow down and take the time to observe your Fire states, you may become aware that your stress thoughts and behaviors always reach a peak around certain people in your life. You may notice that when you hear good news, you usually *do* jump around with excitement, when you never really realized you did that before. You may also start to become cognizant of the fact that you crave and make eye contact differently from others around you. In those moments, you could even become more aware of the skill of imparting hope that you naturally use without even trying.

Step Two:
Understanding Fire's Needs for Safety

You now know how Fire looks and feels when it's strong and when it's stressed, but let's take a look at why primary Fires gets stressed out in the first place.

As Dr. Cowan teaches in the Tournesol Kids #PowerUp program—a nonprofit we created together to teach parents, teachers, and kids the skills for self-awareness, self-regulation, and empathy—we only experience our stress states when our particular needs for safety are not met. Our individual needs for feeling secure are very different and correspond directly to our primary archetype. Just as Fire's strength and stress conditions are unique, so are the particular needs a primary Fire requires to feel balanced and avoid feeling too much stress.

For example, you'll see in the list on the next page that Fire people need a healthy dose of liveliness and passion in their lives. When Fire people go too long without these needs being met, they begin to manifest the stressed behaviors and feelings listed on page 125. However, it's up to them to recognize which of their needs are not being met and make a plan to bring joy, intimacy, and fun back into their lives. If primary Fires were to expect others to fill their lives with passion and liveliness, they would be setting themselves up for disappointment, which leads to panic and anxiety about the people who "ignored" them or "left them out of the fun." Ultimately, expecting others to fulfill your needs for you only drives a wedge in relationships and stokes emotions that make it difficult for you to access your naturally optimistic Fire strengths.

This is why I've created a "needs list" for primary Fires, inspired by what I've learned from Dr. Cowan, so you as an Optimist can better understand your specific needs and spend less time in maladaptive thinking, which leads to discomfort. Recognizing and meeting your individual needs for safety will help you feel courageous, safe, and motivated to cultivate healthy habits and successful relationships.

NOTE: If Fire is not your primary archetype, you can still refer to this Fire's Needs List to better understand and empathize with the primary Fire people in your life. The more skilled you become at empathizing with the needs of others, the more success you'll have in your interpersonal relationships. For more information on how to more harmoniously interact with the other Fire types in your life, turn to page 138.

FIRE'S NEEDS LIST

- Acceptance
- Acknowledgment
- Affection
- Amusement
- Appreciation
- Brightness
- Caring
- Charisma
- Cheer
- Compassion
- Connection
- Contact
- Contentment
- Delight
- Depth
- Diversion
- Emotions
- Encouragement
- Energy
- Enjoyment

- Enthusiasm
- Familiarity
- Feelings
- Friendships
- Fulfillment
- Happiness
- Humor
- Inspiration
- Interaction
- Interest
- Intimacy
- Intuition
- Joy
- Laughter
- Levity
- Liveliness
- Openness
- Optimism
- Passion
- Pep

- Playfulness
- Pleasure
- Rapture
- Reassurance
- Recognition
- Relaxation
- Reward
- Security
- Sensitivity
- Sprightliness
- Stimulation
- Sunlight
- Tolerance
- Touch
- Understanding
- Vibrancy
- Warmth
- Wit

If your primary archetype is Fire, use the needs list to help you:

- Feel relief more quickly in times of challenge.
- Feel less critical of yourself and others.
- Feel more motivated to figure out how to have your own needs met more of the time.

To help you get started, think of a current struggle you're having. Then take a look over the needs list to see if there is a need related to your struggle that you wish you could fulfill right now.

Be mindful that this needs exercise is not about what others aren't giving you or doing for you, as Dr. Cowan teaches. Instead, it's about gaining an awareness of which of your core needs for safety are not being met at that moment and figuring out what *you* can do to have your needs met.

Keep in mind, your individual "needs" work is about empowering yourself to observe how you're feeling and to take control over creating internal harmony. It's about figuring out how you can get your own needs met, not about expecting other people or outside circumstances to change so that you get what you want. I'd be willing to bet you've tried that before and have come up empty-handed. Expecting others to complete us simply doesn't work—sorry, Jerry McGuire!

This is not to say we shouldn't empathize with and care for each other or meet each other's needs within relationships. The sign of a strong relationship is when we can have compassion for and meet each other's shared needs for safety. Take a look back over Neha Chawla's advice for building and nurturing strong relationships on pages 36–38 for a refresher.

Remember that the only thing in this world you can control is you. Take some time to review the needs list that corresponds to your primary archetype. When your stress states creep up, pause instead of reacting. Then practice taking action to acquire the items on the list that you need in your life. Doing so will reduce the frequency and severity of your stress states and allow you to recover from them more quickly and easily. As a result, you'll feel better more of the time and enjoy more fulfilling relationships.

The highest level of having your needs met is being able to meet them for yourself. Being aware of and figuring out how to meet your needs for safety is the way to continuously grow stronger throughout your lifetime. When you're self-aware, self-reliant, empathetic, and empowered to meet your own needs, your life experience is exponentially elevated.

Step Two in the optimization process asks that you recognize which of your specific unmet Fire needs for safety are kicking up your uncomfortable emotions and maladaptive thoughts. The more you practice merely paying attention to your stress and strength states, the easier it will be for you to identify and even predict why you're feeling low. Making this connection subsequently brings you closer to taking control over the seemingly inexplicable ebb and flow of emotions.

For example, a common stress trigger for primary Fires is the feeling of being ignored. When Fire people feel overlooked or forgotten, their biggest fear—of disconnect or loss of love—gets triggered. In the face of their greatest fear, a Fire person may go rapidly into a state of panic, worrying about being cut off when they haven't heard from loved ones, business partners, clients, or friends.

Left to fester, the unchecked emotions that arise from these fear states intensify. In Fire people, this could result in:

+ Worsening anxiety.
+ Distorted levels of panic that are inconsistent with the size of the problem.
+ Too much concern about the possible loss of connection, which backfires, creating more disconnect and exacerbating the problem.

To start practicing Step Two as a primary Fire, examine a current stressor that's bothering you. Next, identify the feelings that arise for you as a result of this specific challenge. These feelings are your need identifiers. Fire types in stress can become exceedingly emotional. They're very sensitive and feel things intensely. In this step, I'm inviting you to pause and observe your emotions as if they're on a billboard you're passing along a highway and not inside you. Instead of allowing your emotions to grow unfettered in response to your challenge, consider that those feelings are only showing up to help you identify your unmet needs for safety. Once you've identified and named the feelings, exhale and ask yourself what unmet need(s) the emotions are telling you that you should focus on from your needs list.

If you're feeling anxious, lonely, or bored, Step Two asks you to notice it. Observe and don't react. Instead, try to see if you can identify what your triggered Fire feelings are telling you that you need in that moment. Are you feeling someone pull away? Are people around you being too serious and not responding to your injection of humor? Have you not gotten any positive feedback in a while from your boss? Are you feeling uninspired by your work?

Any of these examples can dredge up uncomfortable emotions for primary Fire people, but the more you practice gently observing what emotions come up for you in challenging situations, the more you'll remain calm and notice which of your needs aren't being met, instead of spiraling into frenzy and angst.

When you know what is causing your Fire energy to flare up in times of stress, you get closer to becoming resilient to your triggers on a regular basis.

Step Three:
Achieving Balance Within the Fire Archetype

Step Three in the optimization process is about taking action. This is the step for building your foundation of resilience and making new stress-response choices. This is where you begin to build new habits and behaviors, which translate into the creation of new and healthier neural pathways over time and, ultimately, balance within your primary archetype.

Armed with new information about the source of your stressors from Step Two, you're more aware of where your unpleasant feelings are coming from. You understand that they're directly related to whether or not you're having your needs for safety met. Other people and outside circumstances may initiate uncomfortable events, but how you choose to respond is ultimately your decision. If you elect to react while your Fire is unbalanced, you and those around you will spend more time in discomfort.

On the other hand, if your Fire is balanced, you will be more in control of your reactive states under stress and actually reduce the amount of time you and the others spend upset. Reducing your reactivity enables clarity of thought, creativity, smooth conflict resolution, and unconditional love. When you have more control over your stress reactions, you will live a more fulfilling and well-adjusted life.

Let's get to the core of how to achieve a balanced Fire archetype. While Fire is the power of connection, if it's not nurtured and contained properly, it can distort your ability to feel adequately affiliated and relevant in relationships. The Fire archetype needs to support you by contributing its magic instead of its stressed qualities. You also need your Fire to be in harmony so it helps temper and balance out the stress states of the other four types within you. Ultimately, as a primary Fire, your Fire archetype needs to work for you so it can improve your life, instead of making it stressful.

Your Fire-Balancing Skills

Balanced Fire presents itself as the ability to consistently instill hope, even in the face of doubt, and to create a safe space that encourages us and others to share our feelings openly.

As you know, Fire is sensitive and open and seeks to bask in the creative process and live in the moment. But just as the flames of a campfire can easily shift and become unruly if not contained, or instantly be extinguished with too much water, Fire can become hyper and unstable if it doesn't receive a balance of what it needs. Fire's instability can manifest as becoming too silly in times that require a modicum of austerity or overreacting with high levels of anxiety when people don't want to engage or play.

127

We become balanced by taking specific and consistent action that builds and protects the body, mind, and spirit components of our archetypal nature. Eastern well-being philosophies like TCM state that whole health is not achieved by simply addressing one of these three aspects of our overall being. They teach that these three aspects are inextricably connected within us. For example, a physical imbalance causes emotional unrest, which manifests as larger existential conundrums. Consummate balance is the result of a combined effort to empower all three intertwined parts. Thus, you'll notice that the tasks I list for balancing all five archetypes draw upon all three realms: mind, body, and spirit.

✦ ✦ ✦ ✦ ✦

Now that you're familiar with Steps One and Two of the optimization process, in which you learned about Fire's archetypal traits and needs for safety, it's time to learn how to balance your Fire archetype—and even how to help other Fire types do the same.

There are two important ways of doing so:

✦ Self-care in the moment
✦ Long-term maintenance

Fire Self-Care in the Moment

It's important to differentiate between the skills needed for letting off steam in the heat of the moment and those required for building a foundation of resilience to stress triggers over time. As a Fire person, when I'm in the heat of the moment, I'm certainly not naturally inclined to sit down and calmly breathe, organize my thoughts and get quiet, and gently relinquish my heightened emotions.

But in Fire's challenging moments, when panic and anxiety peak, Earth serves as Fire's release valve. Earth activities, behaviors, thoughts, and even people are great at helping Fire fastidiously re-center and gain clarity of mind.

Some Earth tools for releasing the initial pressure include:

+ Asking for help from an empathetic friend who reminds you that he or she is always there for you and that everything will turn out all right.
+ Going someplace where there are people who can help you or just be there to reassure you—instead of being alone.
+ Exhaling, closing your eyes, and identifying where in your body your extreme emotion feels most prominent. Once you've identified the place, imagine what form and color the emotion takes in your mind's eye. Hold that picture in your mind for a moment and then invite it to leave.
+ Eating something nourishing.
+ Speaking to someone whom *you* can help.
+ Sharing a story or a snack with someone.
+ Thinking about three people in your life who have your back and love you unconditionally.

Once you've come down from the peak of your intense Fire stress state, you'll have the composure to mobilize skills from all five archetypes to help you work out the problem that initiated the feelings of insecurity in the first place.

When you, as a primary Fire, feel adequately calm and prepared to begin problem solving, choose the archetype-based activities from the lists on pages 132–37 that correspond to the strengths you most need in the moment. Examples of the strengths that correspond to each type are:

- **Wood:** You'll need to rely on your Wood skills if your problem requires you to fuel up with more motivation—from either a coach or a plan—or if you need to keep your foot on the gas and not give up because you're feeling bored.
- **Fire:** You'll need to draw upon your Fire skills if you need to convince others that everything will turn out well in the end, or if you need to inspire a group of people by giving an entertaining talk or workshop.
- **Earth:** You'll need to access your Earth skills if your issue requires collaboration with others, teaching skills, remembering people's names, or finding out what everyone else wants and needs.
- **Metal:** You'll want to dip into your Metal skills if you're having trouble getting clear about the process for achieving your goals, how you're going to measure your success over time, or if something needs to be edited or better organized.
- **Water:** You'll reach for your Water skills if your issue requires quieting your mind and taking more time to think things through, a more thorough evaluation of all the components impacting your challenge, or sitting back and really listening to everyone's concerns.

Fire Long-Term Maintenance

Another way to achieve balance in your Fire archetype is to practice maintenance activities over the long term to help ensure you remain resilient in the face of stress as you progress. With a stable, reliable cache of resilience accumulated, you will more adeptly wield the skill of observing your challenges rather than reacting to them. The better you become at avoiding reactive states, the more quickly you recover from stress and return to enjoying life.

Begin your maintenance regimen by practicing activities that support your primary Fire archetype. Start by choosing one or two activities from the Fire list to practice every day.

Next, identify one or two activities from the archetype list that correspond to the archetype in which you scored the lowest. Add these items to your daily Fire archetype routine. Don't forget, it's important to practice your lowest archetype, even if it's your least favorite type of activity (which I'm willing to bet it is). Exercising your most vulnerable archetype minimizes the gap between your highest and lowest archetypes, expanding your ability to be more emotionally dexterous when challenges arise.

Finally, practice activities that correlate to the challenges you're currently facing. Here are some examples to help you identify which archetypal skills in the lists on pages 50–59 you will need and will find most helpful as a primary Fire:

+ If you need to stand up for yourself but are afraid you might alienate someone in the process, add in some Wood-building activities.
+ If you need to do a better job remembering people's names and other details of their work or personal lives, beef up on the Earth growth skills.
+ If you keep forgetting small but important details and are making too many typos in your emails, it's likely time to exercise your Metal skills.
+ If you have too much on your plate to give anything the time and energy it deserves, empower your Water abilities.

Choose from among these Fire activities to get you started on building your Fire maintenance regimen:

+ Make time to nurture intimate connections with the people you love on a regular basis. Schedule outings and phone calls, and write letters and emails. Don't get so caught up in your to-do list that you risk feeling disconnected from your support system.
+ Laugh every day, even if it's at yourself in your bathroom mirror.
+ Develop your intuition. You're a natural at it! Observe how you feel around different people and pay attention to your intuitive hits. Do you feel drained, energized, sick, inspired?
+ Recognize when you're avoiding tasks you feel are monotonous or boring.
+ Track which people and situations trigger your panic and anxiety without judging yourself for becoming triggered. Just pay attention to it in the moment so you can have more control over your anxiety in the future.
+ Consider joining a laughter yoga class or an improvisational/stand-up comedy class.
+ Name the emotions that are coming up for you at different times during the day (just name them; you don't have to do anything about them). This reminds you that feelings and emotions fluctuate and are meant to help you identify your unmet needs for safety, as well as which archetypal skills you need to enhance.
+ Smile. Smiling is said to stop the flow of cortisol, the stress hormone.

+ Get a hug from someone you love.
+ Listen to or watch a short comedic sketch that you find funny.

Earth-Building Activities

+ Build and nurture a community of kind, trustworthy people around you, and engage with them regularly.
+ Consider joining a group activity class like dancing, singing, or cooking.
+ Teach someone else a new skill, and bask in the joy of being seen, recognized, and appreciated for helping.
+ Volunteer or do work that inspires others to improve, become more hopeful, and grow stronger.
+ Practice identifying what someone in your life needs, and take care of that need for them for the sole purpose of being compassionate.
+ Make sure you're eating well and that you have healthy digestion. Recognize when you aren't making the best eating decisions because you're solely relishing in the pleasure of what you're eating. Find one item or meal to eat mindfully each day, appreciating every bite, chewing slowly, and pausing between bites. Consider trying to chew twenty times per bite.
+ Find a cause for which you feel particularly passionate and get on board. Use your amazing leadership and inspiration skills to help propel the message forward.
+ Close your eyes and bring your awareness to your body. Can you identify where your current stress sits in your body right now? Observe, breathe into that spot, and exhale with strength through your mouth, imagining that the exhale is releasing the tough emo-

tions through the spot on your body where you envisioned your stress.

+ Practice asking others how they're doing for the sole purpose of building a connection and showing you really care about them. Get granular. Remember details they've shared, and follow up with them on those specific situations.

Metal-Building Activities

+ Metal corresponds to the sense of smell. Use aromatherapy at home and at work, if appropriate. Aromas that support balanced Fire include:

+ Eucalyptus	+ Orange	+ Myrrh
+ Rose	+ Yarrow	+ Viola
+ Cedar wood	+ Lavender	+ Spikenard
+ Frankincense	+ Sandalwood	+ Blilbanum
+ Marjoram	+ Bergamot	+ Lotus

+ Choose or create a handful of your own rituals that you practice regularly and that mean something to you.
+ Set a goal for recognizing and overcoming stress triggers, and come up with a strategy for tracking your success. Reward yourself for staying on target.
+ Practice something that requires coordination and focus to get better, like playing a musical instrument or creating a painting or sculpture.
+ Create a morning routine that you like, build in some flexibility, and then do your best to stick to it.
+ Create and implement a bedtime routine.

+ Find a few breathwork practices you like, and see if you can choose one of them to do once per day.
+ Build in time for a gratitude practice, thinking of things and people in your life for whom you're grateful and why.
+ Arrange your day and month so you don't get too caught up in what's fun in the moment, forsaking what's important for the long term.
+ Keep your office and home neat and at least somewhat organized, even if you have to enlist the help of others to make it happen.
+ Observe self-defeating and anxious thoughts that arise about yourself, others, and situations. Observe them, and then see if you can practice letting them go with a firm exhale.
+ Look around the room and name five things you see. This helps you appreciate and stay in the present instead of getting frustrated about not moving fast enough out of feeling sad emotions.
+ Participate in self-care that gives you personalized attention, like acupuncture or Ayurveda.
+ Establish a dedicated space in your home for a quiet moment of reflection and appreciation each day. Be creative! This could be an elaborate shrine or simply a candle, photos of people you love, or mementos of times and places that hold special meaning.

Water-Building Activities

+ Find time for a few minutes of quiet each day. You could:
    + Practice a fire-gazing meditation.
    + Journal.
    + Take a bath.
    + Read a good book just for fun.
    + Massage your hands and feet with coconut oil before bed.
    + Rest quietly for a few minutes with one hand held over your heart and the other over your abdomen.
+ Try to get to bed before midnight—closer to 10:00 p.m. is even better.
+ Make sure you're drinking enough water each day.
+ Listen to soothing music or calming nature sounds.
+ Start a meditation practice. Make sure it allows for some flexibility and variety because Fire people don't love being alone all that much and have a tendency to get bored with repetition.
+ Go for a swim.
+ Reflect on past times when you became overly anxious about a possible problem and in the end everything turned out fine.

Wood-Building Activities

+ Surround yourself with soothing colors like red, green, violet, or pink.
+ Get a massage.
+ Exercise each day. Come up with a variety of exercises you can do throughout the week that you like. Fire

isn't a huge fan of routine, so mix it up and make it exciting.

+ Make short-term goals for each week so you can fan the flames of your inspired spirit and move toward achieving your dreams and aspirations.
+ Go outside and be in nature. Hug a tree! Literally change your current perspective.
+ Plan your immediate next steps for an item on your to-do list.
+ If you're feeling unmotivated to move an unfinished project forward, imagine how you're going to feel when it's complete.
+ Cultivate a home garden or plants in your space.
+ Plan an adventure, a vacation, or a fun outing.

Ultimately, your Fire archetype is balanced when you:

+ Become more comfortable listening rather than filling space by talking.
+ Begin to take your time getting to know people before jumping into relationships.
+ Pause and contemplate the possible implications of your actions more readily, such as how you might feel after eating an entire tub of ice cream.
+ Are not quite as intensely hyperactive when you hear exciting news.
+ Recall people's names with more ease.
+ Feel inspired and help inspire others more of the time.
+ Actively empathize with your own needs and those of the people in your life.
+ Are aware of your strength and stress states.

+ Know your needs for safety.
+ Are able to predict triggers and recover with ease in times of stress more of the time.
+ Feel confident about your "out of the box" ideas more of the time.
+ Can balance your sense of fun and excitement with staying grounded and completing tasks.
+ Are less bored by the idea of finalizing and refining all the minor details of a project.
+ Don't need to feel entertained or stimulated all the time to feel happy.
+ Are able to fall asleep easily and feel rested when you wake.
+ Are better able to manage your emotional states.
+ Are honest and assertive about your needs and not worried about whether people will like you when you ask to have those needs met.
+ Are better able to evaluate whether particular projects or people are a good investment of your time.

Harmonization

I don't want to leave you hanging, wondering when and how you'll know you're in harmony as a primary Fire.

Again, harmonization is not an absence of stress and challenge. For primary Fires, it's about being able to navigate the challenging moments of your own life while supporting those around you whose Fire archetype may be low and in need of a boost. At its core, harmonization allows you to have unconditional love for yourself and those around you.

When you, as a primary Fire, are harmonized, you're likely to experience many, if not all, of the attitudes and behaviors noted below.

+ You consistently notice, honor, and take control over the connections
  + between how much fun you have and your ability to take adequate time out to rest and replenish.
  + between how much time you spend helping others and how quickly you can de-escalate your feelings of panic.
  + between how organized you are and your ability to avoid feeling anxiety over what has to get done, or what you need to fix.
  + between the amount of water you drink, as well as the time you spend slowing down and the quality of the decisions you make.
  + between the daily goals and agendas you make and your ability to feel motivated to keep moving even when situations are challenging or when you begin to feel bored.
+ You are not as easily distracted by your own thoughts or your inability to sit for prolonged periods of time working on one task.
+ You have more empathy toward people who usually push your buttons.
+ You are not as singularly driven by the need to be loved.
+ You have an easier time focusing on activities that you don't enjoy very much.
+ You are mindful of how your Fiery style of interaction impacts those around you.
+ You are more apt to structure how you spend your time without fear of hurting someone else's feelings.
+ You are better able to consistently trust your own intuition.

FIRE IN RELATIONSHIPS

As our personal awareness and resilience in the face of stress expands, we are less triggered by other people's opinions and tendencies. We also become less likely to attach to relationships that don't serve us well or in which our needs for safety aren't being met. As we strengthen our individual Five Archetypes skills, we are better equipped to form equally strong bonds with individuals from any one of the Five Archetypes, because we see the benefit and the beauty of the gifts they each bring to the companionship.

In this section, primary Fires will gain guidance for building and maintaining propitious relationships, and non-primary Fires will learn how to engage in healthy relationships with primary Fire types.

If You Are a Fire/Optimist

To be a consistently stable Fire partner in any relationship, practice staying in balance by knowing your strengths, challenges, and needs, and by practicing the Fire long-term maintenance activities beginning on page 132. This will ensure that you approach relationship challenges from a place of calm compassion for yourself and your companions.

When you commit to doing the work for keeping your primary Fire in balance, you contribute the following strengths to your interpersonal relationships:

+ Sympathizing with someone else's needs.
+ Helping someone overcome fear.
+ Supporting someone who is healing from grief.
+ Being sensitive to subtle relationship changes that need to be addressed.
+ Bringing fun to relationships.
+ Having compassion for someone else.

- Loving your partner deeply.
- Maintaining a consistent and strong connection.
- Engaging easily.
- Entertaining and keeping things lively.
- Holding deeply intimate conversations.
- Giving and receiving loving physical connection.

When your primary Fire is balanced, you also possess the following characteristics that benefit the global community:

- The desire to create a world devoid of suffering.
- The idealism needed to envision the possibility of something better.
- The ability to passionately recruit others to the cause.
- The drive to respond quickly to fix problems.
- The inspiration and compassion to start a nonprofit organization.
- The energy to keep others lovingly engaged in a mission for the long haul.

On the other hand, when your primary Fire is unbalanced, it shows up in your interpersonal relationships as:

- An inability to sympathize with someone else's feelings.
- Difficulty finding the strength to cheer others up.
- Being aloof to subtle relationship changes that need to be addressed.
- Feeling afraid when others address challenges with you.
- Avoiding sad feelings within relationships at all costs.

- An inability to access your intuition about your partner's needs.
- Rushing into a relationship too fast.
- An impaired ability to engage with ease.
- Fear of being ignored.
- Feeling happiness only when feeling pleasure.
- Fear of losing love and connection.
- Over-smiling, giggling, or laughing to fill uncomfortable silences in conversation.
- Vacillating between being highly engaged and too quiet.

When your primary Fire is unbalanced, watch out for these potential behaviors that could manifest and affect your global community:

- You can't easily access your innate ability to come up with creative ways to curtail people's suffering.
- Your normally idealistic view of a better world is skewed.
- Your ability to encourage others to support a good cause is challenged.
- You don't believe in your amazing ability to fix problems.
- You only feel confident about your work when you receive approval from your staff, supervisor, or other important stakeholder.
- You have a hard time accessing your inspiration and compassion for helping those in need.
- You struggle to lovingly engage communities in a positive mission.

If You Have a Relationship with a Fire/Optimist

In the following pages, you will learn how primary Fires exhibit themselves at work, in intimate relationships, and as parents. Remember, *The Five Archetypes* is a primer for beginners, so I'm just touching on the basic concepts to help you understand, evaluate, and adjust the flow of the primary Fire archetype within you for the best personal and interpersonal outcomes.

The Fire Employee or Coworker

When applied to the workplace, the Five Archetypes method expands your ability and the ability of your coworkers to get things done efficiently. Moreover, when employees and colleagues feel safe, seen, understood, and appreciated in the workplace, they navigate challenges more easily and therefore are less reactive when in stress states, which ultimately translates to a healthier bottom line.

To enhance your awareness of times when your Fire staff or coworkers feel safe and when they feel insecure, there are some common tendencies to watch out for. When you see your colleagues exhibiting their insecure states, it's time to pause and fortify yourself so you don't jump into your reactive states as a result. Get to know these common strengths, needs, and stress states:

> ◆ Strengths at Work: Fire injects joy, optimism, and excitement into a work environment. Fires are warmly receptive to new ideas and changes. They also have an ability to tap into intuitive decision-making skills and are an all-around pleasure to be with.
> ◆ Needs at Work: Fire needs fun, positive feedback; recognition; and opportunities for building and maintaining close relationships.

+ Potential Challenges and Stress States: Unbalanced Fire has a tendency to take on too much, becoming at risk for burnout. Under stress, Fires can become apprehensive and overly silly. Fire people may only gravitate toward projects they feel are fun; they tend to leave the meticulous work for last or ask someone else to do it.

+ Here's how to nurture Fire employees over time and how to help them release tension in challenging moments.

    + Support in the Moment: Meet with your stressed Fire employee or coworker when she feels panicked and anxious and encourage her to share how she's feeling, and remind her that you and the team have her back.

    + Ongoing Encouragement: Regularly coach your Fire employee or colleague with an agenda and plans for how she'll grow with a project in the short term and as a valued team member going forward.

The Fire Friend

Enjoying mutually gratifying friendships starts with *you* knowing how to be a good friend to others. To consistently show up as a steady, sincere, reliable friend, check out these Five Archetypes guidelines:

+ Learn your primary archetype strengths, challenges, and needs so you can practice becoming and staying self-aware.

+ Make sure your needs for safety are being met within the relationship.

+ Recognize and take responsibility for your reactive

states and practice your self-regulation techniques.

+ Adopt a mind-set in which challenge is an invitation to grow, not an excuse to judge or criticize others.

+ Discover your friends' needs for safety so you can practice compassionate consideration.

How Do We Nurture Lasting Friendships?

As a friendship grows, how do we continue to nurture and strengthen our bond using the Five Archetypes method? When you know your friend's primary archetype, you will better understand what makes her feel safe and what makes her insecure. Here are some additional suggestions for what primary Fire people will likely appreciate in a close friendship.

Fires like spending time with people who:

+ Enjoy intimate conversation with them. Fires like to go deep pretty fast.
+ Like excitement and join them in fun activities.
+ Pay close attention to them and sustain eye contact.
+ Would pick up and go out at the drop of a hat.

Helping a Fire Friend in Stress

When you care about someone, you sympathize with their pain and want them to feel better. The Five Archetypes model helps us understand that people have unique stress triggers and also have different paths to de-stressing. Here's how to help your primary Fire friends recover more quickly from stress states.

Draw a Fire friend out of stress mode by empathizing with what she's feeling, reminding her you have her back and that you're right there with her. Once she feels a sense of calm beginning to return, spend some time with her outside, going for a walk and engaging her in a future-focused conversation about next steps.

The Fire Romantic Partner

Primary Fire people bring a sense of playfulness to the union. Your Fire partner will delight in touch, attention, passion, and intimacy. If she's not tired, bedtime is for being close and intimate, whether through a conversation recalling the high points of your relationship or through cuddling and more. She shares her feelings with ease and encourages you to do the same. She has no qualms about PDA, holding you close in public and unabashedly kissing you on street corners.

When Fire types feel insecure, they exhibit specific patterns of disharmony in a relationship. Stressed Fires fear losing love and connection, and panic when they feel ignored by their partner. When things aren't fun anymore and the relationship loses steam, an insecure Fire may feel overburdened by the hard work required to fix issues.

Here are some tips for how you can be a strong partner to a primary Fire type.

+ Do: Tell her you love her regularly. She'll also like being playful and having frequent hugs and kisses (just sayin'...).
+ Don't: Be too serious too much of the time or ignore her. Touch base and tell her you're there, especially when you need to spend time alone processing your own feelings.
+ Help the Fire Person Refocus in Stress: Be present for her and remind her you'll get through rough patches together. Invite her to cook a meal with you. The joint activity will remind her she's an important part of your life.

+ Best Form of Consistent Encouragement: Keep active with your Fire partner. Make plans for the future and fulfill them so she knows you're working toward a goal as a cohesive team.

The Parent–Fire Child Relationship

Your parent-child relationship is impacted not only by the intersection between your and your child's primary archetypes but also by how you perceive your purpose as a parent. When you see your parental role as compassionate guide and teacher and empower your kids to master life skills so they become strong, resilient adults, you're more likely to build a strong relationship with your child and feel fulfilled by the parenting journey.

To create a gratifying and lasting relationship with your primary Fire child using the Five Archetypes method, start by identifying and balancing your own primary archetype. Get to know yourself in strength and in stress. Understand your button pushers so that you're best able to remain in a state of resilience and compassionate power when faced with your triggers. You'll be the most outstanding advocate for and nurture a respectful, strong relationship with your child when you serve as a heroic example of how to manage stress, triggers, and disappointment.

Then find out your child's primary archetype. Help her become more self-aware and self-reliant by teaching her how to recognize and celebrate her gifts. Empower her to overcome stress states with ease by understanding what pushes her buttons and giving her the Five Archetypes tools to become more resilient to her triggers.

Dr. Cowan is a pioneer of using the five types as a methodology for healthy child development. Here are some points, inspired by his work, to keep in mind when parenting a child whose primary archetype is Fire:

+ Learning style: Fire kids learn by feeling and intuition.
+ Sleeping: Fire kids may be afraid of the dark and

may not want to go to sleep for fear of missing out on something more fun than going to bed.

+ Eating: Fire kids like to eat for pleasure because food is simply delicious, so incorporate some education around healthy food habits.

+ Exercise: Fire kids may become bored with repetition, so involve them in the creative decision-making process for coming up with different options to stay active and moving.

+ Feelings: Fire kids feel things very intensely. Not only do they experience their own feelings very strongly but they also naturally absorb and sympathize with the emotions and experiences of those around them. Make sure kids differentiate between their own emotions and those of others and that they understand that feelings are constantly in flux, so they don't make decisions to take action in states of heightened emotion.

FIRE AYURVEDIC PRACTICES

Fire people crave variety in their wellness activities. They'll get bored doing the same activity over and over. If you're a primary Fire, you may prefer to go to a few different places for movement classes, practice more than one option for spiritual growth, study various nutrition philosophies, use assorted health-focused apps, or even sample a diverse variety of creative arts or performance classes.

Primary Fire types will also benefit from regular meditation and will likely crave the solitude of private meditation some of the time, but, again, Fires may find it difficult to stick with a regular practice. A common Fire pitfall is only gravitating toward things that are fun. However, devoting time to a meditation practice helps protect Fires from burnout and quick leaps into anxiety and panic. Additionally, Fires may be more inclined to stick to a meditation practice if they have access to an array of choices for different types of meditation and perhaps different times for practicing during the day. Ultimately, if you focus your wellness pursuits on creating options that are fun and varied, you will more likely stick to the program.

With regard to incorporating Ayurvedic wellness practices into your everyday life, remember that the Fire archetype corresponds to both the fourth and the seventh Chakras.[6] In the chart on the following pages, you will find some gentle Ayurvedic practices that will help engage and balance these chakras.

The fourth Chakra is known as the Heart Chakra. According to Ayurveda, the Heart Chakra relates to romantic love and love for all humankind. The seventh Chakra is known as the Crown Chakra and relates to intuition and spiritual connectedness. Both chakras are directly linked to the joyous, optimistic, and intuitive Fire archetype.

Using Ayurvedic practices is a safe and empowering option to complement any health-care regimen. Peruse the Ayurvedic lifestyle practices below that correspond to your primary Fire archetype. Feel free to try the ones that feel like a good fit as you assemble your menu of healthy lifestyle activities.

---

6   Christopher R. Chase, "The Geometry of Emotions: Using Chakra Acupuncture and 5 Phase Theory to Describe Personality Archetypes for Clinical Use," *Medical Acupuncture* 30, no. 4 (August 1, 2018): 167–78, https://www.ncbi.nlm.nih.gov/pmc/articles/PMC6106753/.

Fourth Chakra— Heart	Seventh Chakra— Crown
Oversees: Romantic and humankind love, relationships, emotions, intuition, group consciousness, kindness, affection, harmonious friendships, spirituality	Oversees: Spiritual and universal consciousness, enlightenment, dignity, vitality, determination, psychic awareness, motivation, passion and excitement, open-mindedness, intelligence, thoughtfulness, understanding, inner light
Location: Heart, right brain, thymus gland, blood, heart, lungs, circulation	Location: Top of the spinal cord, brain stem, pineal gland, right eye, crown of the head
Color: Green	Color: Violet
Mantra: Yam	Mantra: Om
Yoga: Bridge pose, upward-facing dog, bow pose	Yoga: Balancing poses that bring awareness to the body and the mind, like sitting in yoga mudra
Gemstones: Rose quartz, green aventurine, green jade	Gemstones: White jade, diamond, Herkimer diamond, clear quartz
Mudra (a hand gesture that's said to stimulate a specific sense of focus and balance): Pran mudra	Mudra (a hand gesture that's said to stimulate a specific sense of focus and balance): Bhudy mudra

Fourth Chakra—Heart	Seventh Chakra—Crown
Foot marma (a pressure point that's said to enhance mind-body balance when massaged): Point on outside of the bottom of the foot, one inch below the pinky toe	Foot marma (a pressure point that's said to enhance mind-body balance when massaged): Point on the top of the big toe
Aromatherapy: Eucalyptus, rose, cedar wood, frankincense, marjoram, orange, yarrow, lavender, sandalwood, bergamot	Aromatherapy: Frankincense, myrrh, viola, sandalwood, lavender, spikenard, blilbanum, lotus
Taste: Sweet	Taste: Sweet

A Final Note to Primary Fires

Dear Fire Friends,

A few words of passionate enthusiasm as you dance into the world with a fresh Five Archetypes perspective on life:

Remember, your desire to entertain and make people happy can keep your relationships at surface level and hold you back from exploring the deeper meanings of the bonds you so deeply desire. Pay attention to times when you want love and adoration more than you want to hear the truth about how someone feels. Consider taking a peek at the uncomfortable moments you avoid for the chance that they may reveal pathways to even more sublimely satisfying relationships and experiences.

You are an outstanding source of light. When people need a reason to believe in possibility and potential, you have a knack for making them feel encouraged. You're skilled at making everything fun, even on the rainiest of days. I am indebted to you for:

+ Cheering me up when I'm down in the dumps.
+ Embracing me with deep, intimate conversations about feelings and emotions.
+ Being the absolute best childhood friends by eating tons of chocolate-chip cookie dough and giggling all night and chasing dreams about falling in deep, passionate, delicious love.

I wrote a haiku for you in honor of the gifts you bestow upon the world.

> Ignite the whole room
> All eyes on you when you smile
> Keep us filled with joy

With supreme love,
Carey

EARTH

THE CAREGIVER

If you scored highest in Earth traits on your assessment and have confirmed that your results are accurate, then Earth is your primary archetype.

When Earth is your primary archetype, its kindness directs the way you interact with your environment. You share the gifts of empathy, unity, commitment, and devotion with the world.

Earth is the feeling of wholeness that emanates from your center when you know you've improved someone else's life. It's the expansiveness that unfolds in your heart when you cook a nourishing feast and bask in the glow of everyone feeling satiated.

Primary Earth types love to host game night, Thanksgiving, backyard barbecues, and everything in between. Their fridge is always stocked just in case someone drops by unannounced. They love that you rely on them for advice, a cup of sugar, or an extra bedroom when your out-of-town company doesn't all fit at your house. They remember your name, your birthday, your kids' names, and even their birthdays. They're also likely to overcommit because saying no to you is worse than having too much to do.

Earth is the energy of letting others go first and stepping aside to make room so everyone can fit into the circle of conversation. As the "glue" in friendships, primary Earths are exhilarated by the idea of caring for you. Pleasing you is deeply satisfying and inculcates Earth types with a profound sense of self-worth.

The Earth archetype, also known as "The Caregiver," is associated with contribution, appreciation, and togetherness, meaning people who are primary Earths will seek out opportunities to be part of a committed team and crave the process of nurturing ideas and projects that help people and companies thrive. On the flip side, Earth's typical lifestyle challenges revolve around reducing the worry and overwhelm related to fitting in and pleasing everyone, and overcoming the fear of abandonment.

If Earth is not your primary archetype, you will still have some amount of Earth in your nature, so in order to achieve and maintain harmony throughout your lifetime, it's essential that you know where your Earth ranks with respect to the other four archetypes and that you practice the skills that help the Earth in your nature remain strong. The long-term maintenance practices on pages 174–75 will help you both optimize your primary archetype and harmonize your overall nature. They will help you build compassion for yourself and others, as well as a firm foundation of resilience in the face of stress. If Earth is your primary, practicing your long-term maintenance activities will naturally position you to notice and curtail obsessive thinking in times of stress and will increase your ability to foster the growth of healthy relationships and exciting projects. If Earth is your lowest, practicing these activities will naturally help you appreciate the value in networking and building connections with people.

When Earth Is Your Primary Archetype

If Earth is your primary or is tied as one of your two primaries, then this chapter applies most directly to you and how you understand and empower yourself and your relationships.

As a primary Earth, your desire and ability to keep people together and feeling cared for is beyond compare. You have unwavering access to the most compassionate behaviors. When you're on top of your game, your friends, family, and community regard you as a dependable, benevolent guide who takes good care of yourself and others. However, when you're not feeling your best, insecure Earth worries and behaviors prevail, and you may not be able to be your most capable self.

Primary Earth types live their highest spiritual purpose through nurturing cohesive connections and helping others do the same. With genuine interest and care, they check in with other people, asking them how they're doing. Earths will remember the details shared and follow up later on to check on how things have progressed. This is how they show love. They seek to saturate casual conversations with empathy, demonstrating genuine compassion for others. Earth types, at their best, want to express to others that spending time focusing on other people's needs is worthwhile. Earths hope that as a result of these efforts, others will begin to model consideration for people around them by emulating these Earth archetype behaviors.

Earths who feel grounded, self-aware, and secure in who they are will embody distinct traits in their physical, mental, and spiritual being. Physically, Earth types take steps to maintain healthy digestion and good eating habits. Mentally, Earth types remain present in conversation with others, sharing and striving to build rapport and create bonds. Spiritually, Earth types embody and impart the gift of compassion, even in the most challenging situations when others around them choose a less tolerant stance.

When your primary archetype is Earth, you'll also exhibit specific inherent capabilities and attitudes. These patterns persist and are expressed in your personal behaviors, the self-care activities you favor, and the way others perceive you.

Here are a couple of basic Earth archetype indicators to be aware of: When feeling resilient, a primary Earth person is driven to consistently create a sense of togetherness and comfort that benefits both themselves and those around them. On the other hand, when feeling insecure, the Earth type experiences strong feelings of overwhelm and becomes preoccupied with fitting in.

Spending too much time ruminating over pleasing others can lead to feeling perpetually stuck, with an inability to move forward with plans and ideas. This is why it's important for Earths to recognize when it's time to self-regulate, rather than react in a maladaptive manner when faced with a challenge. Sometimes we become so caught up in our dysfunctional thoughts and belief patterns that we can't easily distinguish between rightful action and reactive behavior. To help you know when you're in a state of Earth imbalance and are more likely to make a dysfunctional choice, an Earth type should be on the lookout for times when you:

- Over-care for other people.
- Neglect your own needs.
- Obsessively worry about solving interpersonal conflict.

The ultimate outcomes I hope you achieve as a result of practicing the Five Archetypes method as a primary Earth are twofold: self-empowerment and empathy for others. I want you to strengthen your personal resolve. I want you to know your unique brand of Earth-centered resilience so you can exercise it in the face of friction and conflict. When life's influences and forces lead you toward choices and behaviors that feel most Earth-type comfortable, such as taking care of the needs of everyone around you without protecting yourself, I want you to have the awareness to pause and recognize that your comfort zone is not always your sacred path. With time and patience, you'll establish a foundation of insight and understanding for how to maintain your Earth individuality while simultaneously making sure your own needs for safety and growth are met.

When Earth Is Your Secondary Archetype

If Earth is your secondary archetype, it modifies your primary way of engaging in the world, meaning that Earth behaviors and proclivities more often reveal themselves within your character than your lower three archetypal traits, but not as much as your primary traits.

For instance, as a secondary Earth, you may notice that Earth-specific challenges, like being around people who are pushy or people who are too quiet, kick up discomfort for you some of the time. These Earth-typical challenges won't chronically provoke you the way your primary's trials will, but you will likely notice times when you have Earth needs you want met and Earth frustrations you seek to avoid. Arm yourself with the Earth knowledge in this chapter so you have access to Earth-balancing activities when the need arises.

Here are some archetype-based traits you may notice in yourself or others who are secondary Earths:

+ Fire people with secondary Earth will joyously over-care for you and may tend to stay steadfastly by your side even if the relationship is unhealthy. Fires with secondary Earth may hang their hats on the hope that faltering relationships will get better, even when the evidence points toward a slim chance of healthy reconciliation.
+ Metal people with secondary Earth will set better personal boundaries more of the time than people who

are primary Earth. Metals with secondary Earth will enjoy having you over for a meal, delighted in having cooked exactly the right thing, exactly the right way, and in setting an impeccable table.

+ Water people with secondary Earth will quietly and diligently think of many creative and wise ways to solve your problems and make sure they're taking good care of you.

+ Wood people with secondary Earth will push you to be your best; they want to spend time connecting and talking to you, while also coaching you to meet your goals.

When Earth Is Your Lowest Archetype

Knowing that Earth is your lowest archetype sheds light on the archetype-based skills that may be harder for you to access overall. The scarcity of Earth within your nature will also be more obvious to you in times of stress, when you have a hard time wanting to remain steadfast as part of a team, or when you're in a challenging relationship.

If Earth is your lowest archetype, you may have difficulty empathizing with other people's needs. You may believe that chatting with someone for the sake of growing closer, or offering a kind ear, is not the best use of your time. You may also care much more about getting things done quickly than about checking in with the opinions of others and collaborating to find a solution. Additionally, people who score lowest in Earth may prefer to deal with their issues on their own rather than polling friends about how to move forward. Those with lowest Earth may also believe that focusing on others' problems and concerns is not always the most prudent way to spend an afternoon. They could also have a difficult time trusting other people's intentions.

Having an awareness of your lowest archetype, however, can show you where you need to focus your efforts so you can start building overall resilience to daily stress. Recognizing that Earth is your lowest archetype and doing the work to increase those particular characteristics subsequently propels you to build more rewarding interpersonal relationships; in addition, it improves your ability to get to know and spend time with new people with ease and assurance.

THE FIVE ARCHETYPES METHOD

Optimization

The Five Archetypes method begins with optimization, a process that comprises three steps, which remain the same no matter which archetype is your primary. They are:

1. Recognize your primary archetype's strength and stress states.
2. Understand your primary archetype's individual needs for safety.
3. Achieve balance within your primary archetype.

As a result of optimizing your primary archetype, you will cultivate more empathy and compassion—for yourself and others—and replace old, ineffectual patterns with empowerment. You will embody stability and security in the face of upset. Optimization will also give you elegance and agility at times when you're feeling powerless or tossed about like a rudderless sailboat in response to unpredictable and unstable circumstances—and help you navigate those unchartered waters with more grace and stability.

Step One:
Recognizing Earth's Strength and Stress States

When your Earth archetype is balanced, you will notice that it contributes the strengths of empathy, unity, commitment, and devotion to your life, to your relationships, and to the broader community.

A balanced Earth also helps us:

+ Nourish our bodies with food.
+ Maintain strong, healthy digestion.
+ Remain steadfast in the face of shifting impulses and ideas.
+ Stay committed to responsibilities.
+ Desire to be connected to community.
+ Feel a sense of sustained purpose.
+ Concentrate on managing more than just one thing at a time.
+ Care deeply about remembering people's names.
+ Learn to trust others and to be a trustworthy person.
+ Commit to something and stay the course.
+ Appreciate what skills we need to grow and evolve.
+ Not haphazardly rush through projects, meetings, meals.
+ Nurture lasting relationships.
+ Recognize the benefit of teamwork and collaboration.
+ Know exactly what someone else needs to feel more connected and safe.
+ Teach people skills according to their own learning styles, and not needing others to conform to the way you teach.
+ Provide unwavering support to people who are in need.

We create calm and harmony in our lives and in the lives of others when we have unfettered access to the positive aspects of our Earth. But sometimes our Earth can become unstable, stressed, and unavailable to us. When this happens, we don't feel clear-minded or peaceful, and it's difficult to solve problems for ourselves or in our relationships. Luckily, Earth gives us warning signs to help us know when this is happening.

Stressed Earth manifests as:

+ Obsessing over troublesome things that could potentially happen.
+ Confusion over decision making.
+ Thinking too much about other people's lives.
+ Self-doubt when in social situations.
+ Being hesitant and wishy-washy.
+ Muddled, disorderly thinking.
+ Inability to prioritize.
+ Not setting boundaries and saying yes to things you don't really want to do.
+ Lack of confidence.
+ Digestive problems.
+ Sleep issues.
+ Being too accommodating.
+ Worrying too much about not fitting in.
+ Fear of abandonment.
+ Self-blame.
+ Wondering a lot about what other people think of you.
+ Excessive thinking about what you should do.
+ Inability to prioritize your next steps.
+ Trouble moving forward with your ideas and aspirations.

At its core, recognizing your strong and stressed Earth characteristics in Step One is about shifting how you use your time. Many of us rush through life hoping everything goes well and nothing gets in the way of our ticking off all the items on our to-do list. In such a state, we are more likely to ignore the early signs of internal stress and relationship problems. However, early detection allows us to stave off issues well before they become gnarly, painful situations.

Step One in the optimization process invites you to make time to notice subtle clues that may direct you to course-correct, or perhaps stay right where you are and move a little faster toward your goal.

Start practicing this step by recognizing and tracking your Earth stress and strength states. Recognizing asks you to look and observe, not judge and criticize. There is no right or wrong, good or bad in these states. They're your teachers. They help you know what type of action to take so you continue to develop internal strength and expand healthy relationship skills. So just notice behaviors, like whether or not you chose to ask a new colleague about their family, or if you felt confused or worried because they didn't reciprocate with questions about yours. Become aware of when you're trying to over-please others in spite of what you need and want. Familiarize yourself with these things, and remember to simply pay attention to your Earth tendencies.

Once you get used to noticing when and how your Earth states make themselves apparent in your daily life, you may also choose to track your symptoms or challenge states. Many people become pleasantly surprised at how easy it becomes to take more control over their less pleasant states and to self-regulate simply by taking a little time to notice subtle motivations and feelings.

Over time, you may surprise yourself by spotting patterns of thoughts and behaviors you usually miss when simply rushing through your day. When you slow down and take the time to notice your Earth states, you may become aware that your stress thoughts and behaviors always reach a peak around certain people in your life. You may notice that when people more regularly seek you out for support and enjoy hearing your advice, your ability to allow difficult challenges to roll off your back improves. You may also start to become cognizant of the fact that you honor friendships, loyalty, and honesty differently from others around you. In these moments of heightened awareness, you may more deeply appreciate the impact of your natural proclivity toward unity, togetherness, and caring. These are gifts that Earth types naturally exude without much focused effort.

Step Two:
Understanding Earth's Needs for Safety

You now know how Earth takes form within you when it's strong and when it's stressed, but let's look at why primary Earths get stressed out in the first place.

As Dr. Cowan teaches in the Tournesol Kids #PowerUp program—a nonprofit we created together to teach parents, teachers, and kids the skills for self-awareness, self-regulation, and empathy—we only experience our stress states when our particular needs for safety are not met. Our individual needs for feeling secure correspond directly to our primary archetype. Just as Earth's strength and stress conditions are unique, so are the particular needs a primary Earth requires to feel balanced and avoid feeling too much stress.

For example, you'll see in the list below that primary Earth people need a healthy dose of companionship and togetherness in their lives. When Earth people go too long without these needs being met, they begin to manifest their stressed behaviors and feelings more often and have more difficulty self-regulating. However, it's up to them to recognize which of their needs are not being met and figure out how to make community togetherness and group support a consistent part of their lives. If primary Earths were to expect others to fill their lives with affinity and kinship, they would be setting themselves up for disappointment, which leads to self-criticism and judgment. They will ruminate over what they must have done wrong to cause the people around them to pull away instead of creating or maintaining lasting friendships. Ultimately, expecting others to fulfill your needs for you only drives a wedge in your relationships and stokes emotions that make it difficult for you to access your generous and kind Earth gifts.

This is why I've created a "needs list" for primary Earths, inspired by what I've learned from Dr. Cowan, so you as a Caregiver can better understand your specific needs and avoid getting stuck in overwhelmingly negative thoughts about yourself. Recognizing and meeting your individual needs for safety will help you feel strong, grounded, and motivated to set healthy boundaries and take good care of yourself as well as your relationships.

NOTE: If Earth is not your primary archetype, you can still refer to this Earth's Needs List to better understand and empathize with the primary Earth people in your life. The more skilled you become at empathizing with the needs of others, the more success you'll have in your interpersonal relationships. For more information on how to more harmoniously interact with the other Earth types in your life, turn to page 180.

EARTH'S NEEDS LIST

✦ Association	✦ Certainty	✦ Confidence
✦ Being needed	✦ Collaboration	✦ Connection
✦ Belonging	✦ Communication	✦ Consideration
✦ Comradery	✦ Community	✦ Consistency
✦ Caring	✦ Comprehension	✦ Contact

EARTH'S NEEDS LIST (CONTINUED)

- Contemplation
- Conversation
- Empathy
- Encouragement
- Friendship
- Gathering
- Generosity
- Good nutrition
- Harmony
- Inclusion
- Intention
- Involvement
- Kindness
- Kinship

- Loyalty
- Mutual effort
- Network
- Nurturing
- Peace of mind
- Protection
- Purpose
- Reassurance
- Reciprocation
- Reconciliation
- Relationships
- Security
- Significance
- Sociability

- Social networks
- Stability
- Stories
- Strong digestion
- Sustenance
- Tact
- Team
- Thoughtfulness
- Togetherness
- Tolerance
- Trust
- Unity

If your primary archetype is Earth, use the needs list to help you:

- Feel relief more quickly in times of challenge.
- Feel less critical of yourself and others.
- Feel more motivated to figure out how to have your
  own needs met more of the time.

To help you get started, think of a current struggle you're having. Then look over the needs list to see if there is a need related to your struggle that you wish you could fulfill right now.

Be mindful that this needs exercise is not about what others aren't giving you or doing for you, as Dr. Cowan teaches. Instead, it's about gaining an awareness of which of your core needs for safety are not being met at that moment and figuring out what *you* can do to have them met.

Keep in mind, your individual "needs" work is about empowering yourself to observe how you're feeling and to take control over creating internal harmony. It's about figuring out how you can get your own needs met, not about expecting other people or outside circumstances to change so that you get what you want. I'd be willing to bet you've hoped others would change to make your life easier before and have come up empty-handed. Expecting others to complete us simply doesn't work—sorry, Jerry McGuire!

This is not to say we shouldn't empathize with and care for each other or meet each other's needs within relationships. The sign of a strong relationship is when we can have compassion for and meet each other's shared needs for safety. Take a look back over Neha Chawla's advice for building and nurturing strong relationships on pages 36–38 for a refresher.

Remember that the only thing in this world you can control is you. Take some time to review the needs list that corresponds to your primary archetype. When your stress states creep up, pause instead of reacting. Then practice taking action to acquire the items on the list you need in your life. Doing so will reduce the frequency and severity of your stress states and allow you to recover from them more quickly and easily. As a result, you'll feel better more of the time and enjoy more fulfilling relationships.

The highest level of having your needs met is being able to meet them for yourself. Being aware of and figuring out how to meet your needs for safety is the way to continuously grow stronger throughout your lifetime. When you're self-aware, self-reliant, empathetic, and empowered to meet your own needs, your life experience is exponentially elevated.

Step Two in the optimization process asks that you recognize which of your specific unmet Earth needs for safety are kicking up your uncomfortable emotions. The more you practice merely paying attention to your stress and strength states, the easier it will be for you to identify and even predict why you're feeling out of sorts. Making this connection subsequently brings you closer to taking control over the seemingly inexplicable ebb and flow of your emotions.

For example, a frequent stress trigger for primary Earths is concern over the possibility of being left out. When primary Earth people feel disregarded, their fear of abandonment is provoked. In the face of this fear, a primary Earth person may develop a stomachache or go overboard trying to please the individuals they believe are leaving them out.

When left unaddressed, these worrisome emotions intensify. In primary Earth types, this could result in:

+ Increasing sleep problems.
+ Worsening digestive issues.
+ Setting boundaries becoming even more of a challenge.

To start practicing Step Two as a primary Earth, examine a current stressor that's bothering you. Next, identify the feelings that come up for you as a result of this particular challenge. Your emotions are your need identifiers. Earth types have a tendency to react to challenging situations with overwhelming worry about fitting in or being needed. However, I'm asking you to pause with these uncomfortable emotions instead of reacting and consider that your emotions are there to help you identify your unmet needs for safety in this moment. Once you've identified your feelings, pause for a few beats and ask yourself what unmet need(s) the emotions are telling you that you should focus on from your needs list.

If you're feeling anxious, worried, afraid, or distraught, Step Two asks you to notice it. Observe, and don't react. Try to identify what your overwhelmed Earth feelings are telling you that you need in that moment. Are you feeling lonely? Are your friends or coworkers not including you in activities or as part of planning meetings? Are people around you being too pushy or argumentative?

Any of these examples can dredge up uncomfortable emotions for primary Earth people, but the more you practice pausing and observing what comes up for you when you feel distressing emotions, the more you'll remain calm and have easier access to your problem-solving skills. When you shift into observing how your emotions point to your unmet needs for safety, your time spent in worry, obsession, or self-critical thinking is markedly reduced.

When you know what is causing your Earth energy to get caught up in overwhelm, you grow closer to becoming resilient to your triggers on a regular basis.

Step Three:
Achieving Balance Within the Earth Archetype

Step Three in the optimization process is about taking action. This is the step for building your foundation of resilience and making new stress-response choices. This is where you begin to build new habits and behaviors, which translate into the creation of new and healthier neural pathways over time, and, ultimately, balance within your primary archetype.

Armed with new information about the source of your stressors from Step Two, you're more aware of where your unpleasant feelings are coming from. You understand that they are inextricably tied to whether or not you're having your needs for safety met. Other people and outside circumstances may initiate uncomfortable events, but how you choose to respond in challenging situations is ultimately your decision. If you elect to react while your Earth is unbalanced, you and those around you will spend more time in discomfort.

On the other hand, if your Earth is balanced, you will be more in control of your reactive states under stress and will actually reduce the amount of time you and the others spend being upset. Reducing your reactivity enables clarity of thought, creativity, smooth conflict resolution, and unconditional love. When you have more control over your stress reactions, you will live a more fulfilling and well-adjusted life.

Let's get to the core of how to cultivate a balanced Earth archetype. While Earth is the power of generous commitment to relationships, if it's not nurtured and contained properly, it can become difficult to maintain healthy connections with those you love. The Earth archetype needs to support you by contributing its affectionate spirit instead of its apprehensive stressed qualities. You also need your Earth to be balanced so it can help ground and iron out the stress states of the other four types within you. Ultimately, as a primary Earth, your Earth archetype needs to work for you so it can improve your life, instead of making it more stressful.

Your Earth-Balancing Skills

Balanced Earth presents itself as the ability to consistently communicate our own opinions and needs while simultaneously caring for others and creating harmony within the community around us.

As you know, Earths are guided by the need to create and hold space for compassionate cooperation to ensue. But just as earth that becomes too wet or too dry cannot support the proper growth of a plant or tree, the Earth archetype within us can become muddled or disengaged if it doesn't receive the balance of what it needs to feel safe. Earth's instability can manifest as becoming too preoccupied about caring for others or as an inability to move forward with an ingenious idea.

We become balanced by taking specific and consistent action that builds and protects the body, mind, and spirit components of our archetypal nature. Eastern well-being philosophies like TCM state that whole health is not achieved by simply addressing one of these three aspects of our overall being. They teach that these aspects are inextricably connected within us. For example, a physical imbalance is likely to perpetuate emotional unrest, which balloons and can manifest as a larger existential conundrum. Consummate balance is the result of a combined effort to empower all three intertwined parts. Thus, you'll notice that the tasks for balancing all five archetypes draw upon all three realms: mind, body, and spirit.

✦ ✦ ✦ ✦ ✦

Now that you're familiar with Steps One and Two of the optimization process, in which you learned about Earth's archetypal traits and needs for safety, it's time to learn how to balance your Earth archetype—and even how to help other Earth types do the same.

There are two important ways of doing so:

+ Self-care in the moment
+ Long-term maintenance

Earth Self-Care in the Moment

Earth self-care in a moment of heightened stress calls for different skills from those you'll use for building resilience and ultimately balance over time. Faced with a difficult, heated situation, a primary Earth person is not going to have an easy time quieting the mind and imagining creative ways to solve what likely feels like an insurmountable and multidimensional problem. At the peak of an Earth type's overwhelm, they don't feel capable of effortlessly solving their challenges on their own solely with the power of their perceptive insights.

But in Earth's troublesome moments, such as when worry and overwhelm peak, Metal serves as Earth's immediate release valve. Metal activities, behaviors, thoughts, and people are the most likely to help Earth rebalance and recover from an intense stress state.

Some Metal tools for releasing the initial pressure include:

+ Doing a simple breathing exercise. Close your eyes and inhale through your nose. Imagine you're breathing deep down into your belly so you use your full lung capacity. Hold your inhale for four counts and exhale a nice long exhale through your mouth until the lungs are empty. Repeat three to five times.

+ Choosing one small thing to organize, like a drawer or a closet shelf.
+ Doing a very detailed task that requires focused, specific attention.
+ Tapping your hand or foot to the beat of a song.
+ Thinking of very distinct things you're grateful for in your life right now—the more granular, the better.
+ Looking around the room and naming five things you see. This helps you appreciate and stay in the present instead of getting lost in the overwhelming story of your current dilemma.
+ Remembering particular ways you've helped people in the past.
+ Practicing a ritual or reciting a prayer to a higher power that holds meaning for you.

Metal corresponds to your sense of smell. Below is a list of aromatherapy options that may bring you calm in the moment:

+ Bergamot	+ Lemon	+ Clove
+ Chamomile	+ Lavender	+ Cypress
+ Peppermint	+ Rosewood	+ Marjoram
+ Rosemary	+ Cedar wood	+ Myrrh

Once the severe Earth feelings of stress subside, you'll recover the stability to mobilize skills within you from all five archetypes to help resolve the problem that initiated the reactive insecurity in the first place.

When you, as a primary Earth, feel adequately calm and prepared to begin problem solving, choose the archetype-based activities from the lists on pages 174–78 that correspond to the strengths you most need in the moment. Examples of the strengths that correspond to each type are:

- **Wood:** You'll need to rely upon your Wood skills if your problem requires an agenda, a plan, forward movement, or speed.
- **Fire:** You'll need to draw upon your Fire skills if your problem requires charisma, optimism, deepening connections with people, or discussing your feelings.
- **Earth:** You'll need to access your Earth skills if your issue requires collaboration with another party, teaching others a skill, or gaining an understanding of what everyone needs next.
- **Metal:** You'll want to dip into your Metal skills if your concern revolves around developing a new system, holding yourself or someone else accountable, creating a method for measuring your success, or refining and editing a document.
- **Water:** You'll reach for your Water skills if your issue requires more time to think things through, a deeper evaluation of all the components impacting your challenge, or sitting back and really listening to everyone's concerns.

Earth Long-Term Maintenance

Another way to achieve balance in your Earth archetype is to practice maintenance activities over the long term to help ensure you remain resilient in the face of stress as you progress. With a stable, reliable cache of resilience accumulated, you will more adeptly wield the skill of observing your challenges rather than reacting to them. The better you become at avoiding reactive states, the more quickly you recover from stress and return to enjoying life.

Begin your maintenance regimen by practicing activities that support your primary Earth archetype. Start by choosing one or two activities from the Earth list to practice every day.

Next, identify one or two activities from the archetype list that correspond to the archetype in which you scored the lowest. Add these items to your daily Earth archetype routine. Don't forget, it's important to practice your lowest archetype, even if it's your least favorite type of activity (which I'm willing to bet it is). Exercising your most vulnerable archetype minimizes the gap between your highest and lowest archetypes, expanding your ability to be more emotionally dexterous when challenges arise.

Finally, practice activities that correlate to the challenges you're currently facing. Here are some examples to help you identify which archetypal skills in the lists on pages 50–59 you will need and will find most helpful as a primary Earth:

+ If you're stuck trying to make a big decision and are too concerned about pleasing all the parties involved, add in some Wood-building activities.
+ If you find yourself feeling hopeless, wondering whether things will ever improve, practice some Fire activities.
+ If you're having a hard time setting appropriate boundaries and saying no to people, it's time to exercise your Metal skills.
+ If you always feel you're in a rush and are having a hard time solving complex problems, empower your ability to reflect and find calm with some Water abilities.

Choose from among these Earth activities to get you started on building your Earth maintenance regimen:

+ Build and nurture a community of kind, trustworthy people around you, and practice asking for their help. Track what it feels like when you ask for support, but be sure not to judge yourself for experiencing the feelings that arise. Simply observe.
+ Volunteer regularly at a nonprofit whose mission aligns with your personal calling.
+ Observe and track the times you offer support even when you don't want to. Consistently paying attention to these times without judging yourself will help you gain more control over the behavior in the long run.
+ Practice identifying what *you* need once per day, and schedule time to give yourself those things. It could be a reward of ten glorious minutes to yourself, or splurging on a piece of your favorite chocolate, or perhaps taking a walking tour of an area of town you've always been curious about.
+ Make sure you're eating well and that you have healthy digestion. Pay attention to the relationship your body has with your food. Notice whether you feel constipated, gassy, or bloated, or if you have acid reflux. If your digestion feels shaky, seek the guidance of a nutrition specialist to get it back on track.
+ Find one item or meal to eat mindfully each day, appreciating every bite, chewing slowly, and pausing between bites. Consider trying to chew twenty times per bite.
+ Close your eyes and bring your awareness to your

body. Can you identify where your current stress sits in your body right now? Honor what you've observed by pausing with this realization for a moment. Breathe into that spot with an inhale through the nose. Exhale with strength through your mouth, imagining the stress is actually leaving your body through the spot where you envisioned it.

+ Mentor someone or teach a class on a topic about which you're passionate.

Fire-Building Activities

+ Have fun! Build in time to kick back with friends and enjoy pleasant activities together.
+ Practice articulating your emotions, which is a self-nurturing way to deal with feeling stuck and unsettled. Recognize and say how you feel—first to yourself and then to those around you when you feel the confidence to do so. Over time you won't feel as though you're burdening people with your emotions. You'll realize you deserve to be seen and acknowledged too.
+ Try a laughter yoga class.
+ Smile at people—it spreads joy and is said to reduce cortisol production.
+ Practice heart-opening yoga stretches like cow pose, cobra pose, and locust pose.
+ Watch inspirational speakers on video or in person.

Metal-Building Activities

+ Create some structure within your day and do your best to stick to it—whether it's a morning routine, eating meals around the same time each day, creating a bedtime routine, or maintaining a routine for prayer or worship. Come up with a structure for how to measure your success in keeping your routines.

+ Adopt a breathwork practice that you like and do it regularly.

+ Upon waking and right before you fall asleep at night, think of people for whom you're grateful.

+ Track your stress triggers and patterns so you can have more control over them in the future.

+ Participate in self-care that gives you personalized attention, like acupuncture or Ayurveda.

+ Metal corresponds to our sense of smell. Use aromatherapy at home and at work if appropriate. See the list of aromatherapy options on page 171.

+ Choose or create your own ritual that means something to you and practice it regularly.

+ Set a goal for recognizing and overcoming stress triggers and include a strategy for tracking your success. Reward yourself for staying on target.

+ Practice something that requires coordination and focus to get better, like playing a musical instrument or creating a painting or sculpture.

+ Observe negative thoughts that arise about yourself, others, and situations. Observe them and then see if you can practice letting them go with a firm exhale through the mouth.

Water-Building Activities

+ Make sure you're drinking enough water each day.
+ Massage your hands and feet with a little coconut oil before bed each night.
+ Build in time every day to slow down, whether it's by taking a slow walk, journaling, watching a movie, or getting a manicure. Allow your body and mind some time to recover regularly from the caring and worrying you do about everyone else in your life.
+ Listen to gentle, calming music.
+ Read a book you enjoy.
+ Join a meditation class. Make sure it's a practice that feels like a fit for you because Earth people don't always prefer meditating alone.
+ Take a bath with lavender oil.
+ Swim.
+ Try to get to bed before midnight—as close to 10:00 p.m. as possible.
+ Rest quietly for a few minutes with one hand held over your heart and the other over your abdomen.
+ Think of times you've felt left out, or when important relationships ended and you were able to move forward and build even stronger relationships with new people, incorporating the lessons you learned in the past.

Wood-Building Activities

+ Take some time each day to think about what you need and make a plan for how you're going to have your needs met. This can be anything from making sure you eat three meals to asking for help picking up your kids from school.

+ Sign up for an exercise class or create a regular exercise routine. Consider incorporating practices that combine breathing with stretching and moving like yoga, qi gong, or tai chi.
+ Create a list of goals each week and stay on target to complete them. If this is tough for you, start small, with goals that are easy to reach, and over time increase the complexity of the goals you choose.
+ Surround yourself with soothing colors like orange, yellow, and gold.
+ Go outside and be in nature. Hug a tree or touch a plant.
+ Plant your own garden, or buy and nurture some houseplants.
+ Find something at work or at home that you can be in charge of, preferably with delegation responsibilities, so you can practice being in charge.
+ Schedule a regular massage.
+ Plan an adventure, a vacation, or a fun outing.

Ultimately, your Earth archetype is balanced when you:

+ Feel less worried overall about being left out.
+ Are able to say no when you don't have time or energy to support someone else in the moment.
+ Can balance your desire to meet the needs of others with an equal desire to meet your own needs.
+ Feel more comfortable spending quiet alone time to replenish.

+ Have an easier time falling asleep at night and not ruminating about the day's happenings.
+ Are less avoidant of talking about your personal achievements.
+ Blame yourself less when relationships don't work out.
+ Are aware of your strength and stress states.
+ Know your needs for safety.
+ Don't get endlessly stuck in the decision-making process as often.
+ Feel more motivated to exercise regularly.
+ Have strong and healthy digestion.
+ Are less afraid people will jump ship if you say you can't help them.
+ Are able to predict triggers and recover from stress with ease more of the time.
+ Have more drive to bring your ideas to fruition more of the time.
+ Are able to breathe or use other Metal skills to regulate with ease in times of stress.
+ Are led more by what is truly the best option for all parties rather than by the fear of not fitting in with the crowd.
+ Recognize more quickly when your ideas or projects are stagnating because you're fearful of taking an entrepreneurial risk.
+ Are more aware of times when you want to chat for longer than the people around you desire to hold a conversation.
+ Are okay exercising on your own as opposed to needing to be part of a class or group.
+ Don't avoid taking the lead for fear you'll hurt the feelings of someone else who may have wanted to take charge.

Harmonization

I don't want to leave you hanging, wondering when and how you'll know you're in harmony as a primary Earth.

Again, harmonization is not an absence of stress and challenge. For primary Earths, it's about being able to navigate the challenging moments of your own life while empathizing with and supporting those around you whose Earth archetype may be low and in need of a boost. At its core, harmonization allows you to have unconditional love for yourself and others.

When you, as a primary Earth, are harmonized, you're likely to experience many, if not all, of the attitudes and behaviors noted below.

- ✦ You consistently notice, honor, and take control over the connections
  - ✦ between the strength of your digestive system and how quickly you recover from stress.
  - ✦ between staying on a schedule and not getting bogged down in worry.
  - ✦ between the quality of sleep you get and how well you protect your needs in relationships.
  - ✦ between the goals you set for yourself and your drive to complete projects and bring ideas to fruition.
  - ✦ between how easily you recognize the humor in situations that feel challenging and your ability to set healthy boundaries.
- ✦ You cherish spending time alone reflecting on the day.
- ✦ You consistently follow through on and complete initiatives in a timely manner.
- ✦ You don't feel the need to solve other people's problems.
- ✦ You stand up for yourself more.
- ✦ You regularly fall asleep with ease and stay asleep through the night.

- You believe your ideas and suggestions are worth sharing and implementing.
- You more readily let go of relationships that are harmful.
- You spend more time getting to know potential friends and projects and less time fantasizing about being with them forever.
- You don't obsess about hurting other people's feelings.
- You don't concern yourself wondering what other people think of you.

EARTH IN RELATIONSHIPS

As our personal awareness and resilience in the face of stress expands, we are less triggered by other people's opinions, moods, and tendencies. We also become less likely to attach to relationships that don't serve us well or in which our needs for safety aren't being met. As we strengthen our individual Five Archetypes skills, we are better equipped to form equally strong bonds with individuals from any one of the Five Archetypes because we see the benefit and the beauty of the gifts they each bring to the companionship.

In this section, primary Earths will gain guidance for building and maintaining healthy relationships, and non-primary Earths will learn how to engage in outstanding relationships with primary Earth types.

If You Are an Earth/Caregiver

To be a good Earth partner in any relationship, practice staying in balance by knowing your strengths, challenges, and needs, and by practicing the Earth long-term maintenance activities on pages 174–75 to remain a consistently stable partner. This will ensure you approach relationship challenges from a place of calm compassion for yourself and your companions.

When you commit to doing the work that keeps your Earth in balance, you contribute the following strengths to your interpersonal relationships:

+ Desiring to help others succeed.
+ Knowing exactly what others need to feel better.
+ Wanting to serve others and make sure they're content.
+ Being faithful and devoted.
+ Being honest and trustworthy.
+ Mediating a peaceful solution.
+ Having sincerity and forthrightness.
+ Networking and introducing people to one another.
+ Steady dedication in relationships.
+ Helping other people realize their dreams.
+ Communicating compassionately and clearly to solidify bonds.
+ Sharing details about yourself and exhibiting curiosity to know particulars about others.
+ Contributing sweetness, calming, and warmhearted energy to a bond.
+ Enjoying the process of building understanding and trust through the give-and-take of conversation.
+ Striving to make everyone around you feel safe.

When your primary Earth is balanced, you also possess the following characteristics that benefit the global community:

+ The desire to be a part of something admirable.
+ An unwavering commitment to a charitable mission.
+ The inclination to drop everything to right a wrong.
+ The ability to keep a team focused on a singular altruistic goal.

+ The ability to remain committed to a cause even in the face of conflicting personal opinions and goals.
+ The ability to absorb ideas and inspiration and manifest them into practical applications that empower people.
+ The ability to cultivate concepts with a team to help deliver a fully complete project.
+ Dependability and dedication over the long haul.
+ Consistent work to raise awareness for actions that drive a humanitarian mission forward.

On the other hand, when your primary Earth is not in balance, it shows up in your interpersonal relationships as:

+ Being too concerned about fulfilling other people's needs.
+ Avoiding taking care of yourself in a relationship.
+ Becoming a "doormat" and not being able to say no.
+ Oversharing or talking too much.
+ Not being able to teach people.
+ Lacking the ability to nourish others.
+ Misunderstanding people's needs.
+ Getting too involved in other people's drama.
+ Having trouble quieting your thoughts enough to listen clearly to your needs and those of the people around you.
+ A potential for codependent behaviors.
+ Avoiding conflict because you think it's inherently a bad thing.
+ Over-accommodating others' needs for fear they'll leave and you'll be alone.
+ Feeling guilty asking to have your needs met in a relationship.

+ Believing it's your fault when other people aren't getting along.

When your primary Earth is unbalanced, watch out for these potential behaviors that could manifest and affect your global community:

+ Overanalyzing the components of a plan to the point of inactivity.
+ Excessively discussing strategy instead of driving an initiative forward.
+ Worrying that you're not doing enough to help people in need.
+ Becoming confused over the greater purpose of a venture after too much theorizing.
+ Losing sight of your personal goal in favor of supporting everyone else's.
+ Focusing so much on relationships that you lose the impetus to launch your initiatives.
+ Being overly accommodating to the needs of the team.
+ Inconsistently nourishing the community you hold dear due to internal worry about whether or not you're pleasing everyone.

If You Have a Relationship with an Earth/Caregiver

In the following pages, you will learn how primary Earths exhibit themselves at work, in intimate relationships, and as parents. Remember, *The Five Archetypes* is a primer for beginners, so I'm just touching on the basic concepts to help you understand, evaluate, and adjust the flow of the primary Earth archetype within you for the best personal and interpersonal outcomes.

The Earth Employee or Coworker

When applied to the workplace, the Five Archetypes method expands your ability and the ability of your coworkers to get things done efficiently. Moreover, when employees and colleagues feel safe, seen, understood, and appreciated in the workplace, they navigate challenges more easily and therefore are less reactive when in stress states, which ultimately translates to a healthier bottom line.

To enhance your awareness of times when your Earth staff or coworkers feel safe and when they feel insecure, watch for some common tendencies. When you see your colleagues exhibiting their insecure states, it's time to pause and fortify yourself so you don't jump into your reactive states as a result. Get to know these common strengths, needs, and stress states:

- Strengths at Work: Earth staff are caring and sharing. They're good at sticking with a project and giving it the attention it needs over the long haul.
- Needs at Work: Earths want to be involved in projects and needed by the team. They crave togetherness, so make sure they're included in conversations and group lunches. They don't mind leading humanitarian-type efforts, but they're not usually interested in being the center of attention.
- Potential Challenges and Stress States: Under stress, Earths can worry too much about being included or about whether they're being as supportive to the team as needed. Their worry can grow and turn into feeling stuck making decisions. Insecure Earths may spend too much time in the collaborative stage, discussing how things will work and not getting moving on making new projects happen.

+ Here's how to nurture Earth employees over time and how to help them release stress in the moment.

  + Support in the Moment: Redirect your stressed Earth employee or coworker to the structure of the day and the continuity of what's next on the to-do list in order to keep a project organized and moving forward. The focus on the strategic and structural details helps them reduce feelings of overwhelm.
  + Ongoing Encouragement: Nurture a sense of connection over time with your Earth employee or colleague through regular lighthearted and compassionate conversation so he feels like a cherished and important part of the team.

The Earth Friend

Enjoying mutually gratifying friendships starts with *you* knowing how to be a good friend to others. To consistently show up as a steady, sincere, reliable friend, check out these Five Archetypes guidelines:

+ Learn your primary archetype strengths, challenges, and needs so you can practice becoming and staying self-aware.
+ Make sure your needs for safety are being met within the relationship.
+ Recognize and take responsibility for your reactive states and practice your self-regulation techniques.
+ Adopt a mind-set in which you perceive challenge as an invitation to grow, not an excuse to judge or criticize others.

+ Discover your friends' needs for safety so you can practice compassionate consideration.

How Do We Nurture Lasting Friendships?

As a friendship grows, how do we continue to nurture and strengthen our bond using the Five Archetypes method? When you know your friends' primary archetypes, you will better understand what makes them feel safe and what makes them feel insecure. Here are some additional suggestions for what primary Earth people will likely appreciate in a close friendship.

Earths like spending time with people who:

+ Value spending quality time together.
+ Are devoted to the relationship for the long term.
+ Demonstrate that they are appreciated and needed.
+ Involve them in talking through difficult decisions.

Helping an Earth Friend in Stress

When you care about someone, you sympathize with their pain and want them to feel better. The Five Archetypes model helps us understand that people have unique stress triggers and also have different paths to de-stressing. Here's how to help your primary Earth friends recover more quickly from stress states.

Arouse an Earth friend out of worry by reminding him how grateful you and others are for his contributions to your lives. Share with him how terrific he is and how he adds a sense of meaning to everyday experiences. He will also benefit from the time you spend with him, cheering him up and being optimistic about the fact that things will turn out all right in the end.

The Earth Romantic Partner

Primary Earth people bring a sense of connection and security to the union. Your Earth partner will stick with you through thick and thin, diving into your challenging dilemmas alongside you to help you achieve reasonable resolutions. Earth partners are easygoing and gentle. They'll usually let you pick the movie or decide where to have dinner. At night, he'll hold you tight and find delight in talking through the interactions of the day. He'll always want to host dinners with friends and will be the glue that holds the family together.

When Earth types feel insecure, they exhibit specific patterns of disharmony in a relationship. Stressed Earths fear being abandoned by their partner and may over-please to make sure their love doesn't leave. When Earths become stuck in a cycle of stress because their needs for safety aren't being met, they will try to avoid conflict at all costs and may blame themselves when things in the relationship go south.

Here are some tips for how you can be a strong partner to a primary Earth type.

- Do: Have conversations with him about how your day went.
- Don't: Spend a lot more time with your friends than you do with him, or tell him he's crowding you when he wants to talk.
- Help Them Refocus in Stress: Thank him for being such an amazing partner and being so attentive.
- Best Form of Consistent Encouragement: Keep it lighthearted with your Earth partner. Play games for the sake of enhancing your connection, not only to win. He'll love this time with you.

The Parent–Earth Child Relationship

Your parent-child relationship is impacted not only by the intersection between your and your child's primary archetypes but also by how you perceive your purpose as a parent. When you see your parental role as compassionate guide and teacher and empower your kids to master life skills so they become resilient adults, you're more likely to build a strong relationship with your child and feel fulfilled by the parenting journey.

To create a gratifying and lasting relationship with your primary Earth child using the Five Archetypes method, start by identifying and balancing your own primary archetype. Get to know yourself in strength and in stress. Understand your button pushers so that you're best able to remain in a state of resilience and compassionate power when faced with your triggers. You'll be the most outstanding advocate and nurture a respectful, stable relationship with your child when you serve as a heroic example of how to manage stress, triggers, and disappointment.

Then, find out your child's primary archetype. Help him become more self-aware and self-reliant by teaching him how to recognize and celebrate his gifts. Empower him to overcome stress states with ease by understanding what pushes his buttons and giving him the Five Archetypes tools to become more resilient to his triggers.

As you know, Dr. Cowan is a pioneer of using the five types as a methodology for healthy child development. Here are some points, inspired by his work, to keep in mind when parenting a child whose primary archetype is Earth:

+ Learning style: Earth kids learn through stories and context.
+ Sleeping: Earth kids like to talk before going to bed. It helps them sort through and release the various stories and worries that accumulated within them during the day.

+ Eating: Earth kids like to eat together with the family or with friends; they value this time as an opportunity for bonding and connection, exchanging stories and kindness.
+ Exercise: Earth kids may not be the most motivated when it comes to regular exercise, but if they're participating in a group activity or class, they're likely to be more driven to take part.
+ Feelings: When Earth kids are not at their best, they tend to worry a lot about pleasing everyone. It's important to Earth kids that everyone around them is getting along because they feel unsettled in the face of conflict. Make sure your Earth kids understand that feelings are constantly in flux, so they don't feel stuck in states of heightened emotions.

EARTH AYURVEDIC PRACTICES

Earth people participate in wellness activities that reinforce building and maintaining connections with others. They'll most likely prefer taking part in a group class rather than exercising on their own. For example, even though Earth people thrive when they're able to quiet their busy minds through some form of meditative activity, they don't particularly enjoy being alone with their thoughts. For Earths to feel drawn to meditation, it should be either as part of a group or community or a type of meditation that doesn't aim to have the participant spending too much time alone with their thoughts. Other options include walking meditations, candle gazing, and chanting. Earth types can even reach meditative states by immersing themselves in focused activities like jogging, painting, and playing a musical instrument.

Ultimately, if you focus your wellness pursuits on community togetherness, you will more likely stick to the program.

With regard to incorporating Ayurvedic wellness practices into your everyday life, remember that the Earth archetype corresponds to the third Chakra. In the chart on the next page, you will find some gentle Ayurvedic practices that will help engage and balance this chakra.

The third Chakra is known as the Solar Plexus Chakra. According to Ayurveda, the Solar Plexus Chakra governs personal power, which, when in balance, correlates to the Earth archetype's groundedness and ability to be an unwavering support for themselves and others.

Using Ayurvedic practices is a safe and empowering option to complement any health-care regimen. Peruse the selection of Ayurvedic lifestyle practices below that correspond to your primary Earth archetype. Feel free to try the ones that feel like a good fit as you assemble your menu of healthy lifestyle activities.

Third Chakra—Solar Plexus

Oversees: Energy, vitality, desire, power, sense of belonging, mental understanding of emotions, personal will, ego. Also oversees feelings of expansiveness and spiritual growth. Its main quality is peace. This chakra governs personal power, self-assertion, dynamism, generosity, contentment, satisfaction, and expansive consciousness.

Location: Pancreas, stomach, liver, eyes, large intestine

Colors: Yellow and gold

Mantra: Ram

Yoga: Heat-building poses like sun salutations, warrior pose, bow pose, seated twisting hip-openers, boat pose

Gemstones: Citrine, calcite, topaz

Mudra (a hand gesture that's said to stimulate a specific sense of focus and balance): Apan mudra, ahamkara mudra

Foot marma (a pressure point that's said to enhance mind-body balance when massaged): On the outside edge of the foot/pinky toe side, about two inches down from the top of the pinky toe

Aromatherapy: Bergamot, chamomile, lavender, golden yarrow, peppermint, rosemary

Taste: Sour

A Final Note to Primary Earths

Dear Earth Friends,

A few words of support as you contribute to the world with a fresh Five Archetypes perspective on life:

Remember, your commitment to helping others has the potential to keep you from caring for your own needs if your primary Earth archetype is not balanced. You will not be helpful to any of us if you're not feeling well. Carve out time for yourself. I'll bet some self-focus will empower you with even more energy to make the world a better place.

You are an expert at creating stability for all those around you. Your kindness is unmatched, and I can always count on you to know how to make me feel better. I am indebted to you for:

+ Always being there for me when I'm in panic mode and reminding me that I'm not alone.
+ Demonstrating the benefits of collaboration in creating a propitious outcome.
+ Reminding me to elevate my eating experience to a more mindful practice so I'm not as apt to eat the entire sleeve of Girl Scout Thin Mints in one sitting.

I wrote a haiku for you in honor of the gifts you bestow upon the world.

Your caress restores
We are nomads without you
Tell us sweet stories

Your loyal student,
Carey

METAL

THE ARCHITECT

If you scored highest in Metal traits on your assessment and have confirmed that your results are accurate, then Metal is your primary archetype.

When Metal is your primary archetype, its gracefulness directs the way you interact with your environment. You share the gifts of beauty, organization, preparedness, and conscientiousness with the world.

Primary Metal types admire and notice distinct details of a room, a work of art, or a piece of clothing that others may miss. They design their space with intention and precision and deeply appreciate when others notice their good taste. Metals are organized, and they make sure their home is spotless before turning in for the night. They have an impeccable memory and recall exactly where they left the scissors and the extra bottle of olive oil, and which high school yearbook pages have photos of them.

At work, Metal types make sure meetings start and end on time and that all items on the agenda are covered. They ensure that everyone is clear on their takeaways, next steps, and deadlines so the team remains on target with expectations. Metals have perfected their morning and bedtime routines because getting it right guarantees they'll have a productive day. They set a good example by always being true to their word and not getting too emotional when bad things happen. They don't react to displays of anger. Instead, they practice restraint in the hopes that others will learn from their example.

The "discerning" one in friendships, Metal is invigorated when you ask her opinion. She knows the most amazing cardiologist, cleanest nail salon, and most meticulous bookkeeper; she's particular because she's learned from choosing people who weren't the best in the past. Imparting her lessons learned is deeply satisfying and gives Metal types a profound sense of self-worth.

The Metal archetype, also known as "The Architect," is associated with ceremony, meticulousness, and appreciation for mastering skills, meaning that people who are primary Metals believe that practice makes perfect; they flourish within well-established philosophies and systems. On the flip side, Metal's characteristic lifestyle challenges revolve around learning not to get too stuck on details and minutia, and in overcoming self-critical and limiting beliefs.

If Metal is not your primary archetype, you will still have some amount of Metal in your nature, so in order to achieve and maintain harmony throughout your lifetime, take note of where your Metal ranks with respect to the other four archetypes and practice the skills that help keep the Metal in your nature strong. The long-term maintenance practices beginning on page 216 will help you both optimize your primary archetype and harmonize overall, as well as build a firm foundation of resilience in the face of day-to-day stress. If Metal is your primary, practicing your long-term maintenance activities will naturally propel you to feel more emotionally flexible in times of stress, reducing your inclination to get stuck judging yourself for the feelings that come up in frustrating situations. If Metal is your lowest, practicing these activities will help naturally increase your attention to detail, set better boundaries, and help you better appreciate and adequately apply lessons learned from past mistakes.

When Metal Is Your Primary Archetype

If Metal is your primary or is tied as one of your primaries, then this chapter applies most directly to you.

As a primary Metal, your desire and ability to create beauty and a consistent, safe environment for your family, friends, and coworkers is exceptional. You present yourself with a composed and gracious disposition. When you're feeling secure and respected, those who know you regard you as a principled, trustworthy, and devoted advocate. However, when you're not feeling your best, apprehensive Metal states become more prevalent, and you're not able to put your best foot forward.

Primary Metal types live their highest spiritual purpose by demonstrating and sharing exceptional levels of virtue and forgiveness. They distill order and structure from disparate and competing elements to create one whole functioning machine. They demonstrate what it means to continuously improve through practice and preparation. Metal types, at their outright best, want to express to others the value gained through focused and ongoing effort. In a spiritual sense, primary Metals hope that as a result of these efforts, others will follow suit and live a life of virtue, respectability, and strength of character.

Metals who feel grounded, self-aware, and secure in who they are will embody distinct traits in their physical, mental, and spiritual being. Physically, Metal types are outstanding at controlling their breath and using it to achieve calm. Mentally, Metal types like to create and maintain routine, working toward building consistency within which everyone around them can flourish. Spiritually, Metal types embody and share the gift of forgiveness and gratitude, even in the face of chaos and emotional outbursts from those around them.

When your primary archetype is Metal, you'll exhibit specific inherent capabilities and attitudes. These patterns persist and are expressed in your choices, reactions, behaviors, in the self-care activities you embrace, and in the way others regard you.

Here are a couple of basic Metal archetype indicators to be aware of: When feeling resilient, a primary Metal person is driven to build a sense of beauty, function, and standards that set the stage for the comfort of their own environment and that of those around them. On the other hand, when feeling insecure, the Metal type becomes overcritical and judgmental of herself and others, worrying too much about making mistakes.

Spending too much time worrying about whether or not you're wrong impacts your ability to appreciate and focus on the bigger picture when working to achieve creative solutions that support the greater good. This is why it's important for Metals to recognize when it's time to self-regulate, rather than react in a maladaptive manner when faced with challenge. Sometimes we become so caught up in our dysfunctional thoughts and belief patterns that we can't easily distinguish between rightful action and reactive behavior. To help you see when you're in a state of imbalance and are more likely to make a dysfunctional choice, primary Metal archetypes should be on the lookout for times when they:

+ Feel stuck in feelings of grief.
+ Focus too much on small details.
+ Obsessively concern themselves with being right.

The ultimate outcomes I hope you achieve as a result of practicing the Five Archetypes method as a primary Metal are twofold: self-empowerment and empathy for others. I want you to strengthen your personal resolve and know your unique brand of Metal-centered resilience so you can exercise it in the face of friction and conflict. When life's influences and forces lead you toward choices and behaviors that feel most Metal-type comfortable—like judging other people's opinions or ways of accomplishing tasks as inferior—I want you to have the awareness to take a step back and recognize that your comfort zone is not always your sacred path. With time and patience, you'll establish a foundation of insight and understanding for how to maintain your Metal individuality while simultaneously enveloping those around you with compassion and kindness.

When Metal Is Your Secondary Archetype

If Metal is your secondary archetype, it modifies your primary way of engaging in the world, meaning Metal behaviors and proclivities more often reveal themselves within your character than your lower three archetypal traits, but not as much as your primary traits.

For instance, as a secondary Metal, you may at times become agitated by Metal-specific challenges such as a lack of continuity or consistency in communication or disorderly and unclear office structure and policy. These Metal-typical challenges won't chronically provoke you in the way that the challenges associated with your primary will, but you will likely notice times when you have Metal needs you want met and Metal frustrations you seek to avoid. Arm yourself with the Metal knowledge in this chapter so you have access to Metal-balancing activities when the need arises.

Here are some archetype-based traits you may notice in yourself, or others who have secondary Metal:

+ Earth people with secondary Metal will care about pleasing you but will likely have an easier time setting boundaries for themselves and saying no.

- Water people with secondary Metal will spend less time lost in their thoughts or imagination, because the strong Metal supports their ability to more precisely structure their time.
- Wood people with secondary Metal will be more likely to devote time to perfecting the details of a project instead of simply rushing to complete it and sending it out without proofreading. They balance their need to be first with a desire to create a well-designed product.
- Fire people with secondary Metal will be more cognizant of times when they're acting too silly, oversharing, or not respecting other people's boundaries.

When Metal Is Your Lowest Archetype

Knowing that Metal is your lowest archetype sheds light on the archetype-based skills that may be harder for you to access overall. The scarcity of Metal in your nature will likely be more obvious to you in times of stress, such as when you have quickly escalated into feelings of panic or anger in the face of disappointment.

If Metal is your lowest archetype, you may not focus on using your full lung capacity when breathing, and you probably struggle to adequately structure your time, refine projects, organize your living or working space, or recognize when you've shared information that may be inappropriately intimate for the group of people you're with. You may also not care about getting things done perfectly because you're more focused on having a good time or rushing through to the finish line. Additionally, people who score lowest in Metal may have a tough time controlling their emotions and may not feel comfortable setting healthy, appropriate, protective boundaries in relationships. They may come across as careless at times and could have a hard time defining the steps they need to take to accomplish their goals.

Having an awareness of your lowest archetype, however, can show you where you need to focus your efforts so you can start building overall resilience to daily stress. Recognizing that Metal is your lowest archetype and doing the work to increase your Metal characteristics subsequently propels you to build more rewarding interpersonal relationships, improves your ability to discern how best to invest your time, drives you to elevate the mundane moments into something more meaningful, and encourages you to create standards that protect your own needs for safety.

THE FIVE ARCHETYPES METHOD

Optimization

The Five Archetypes method begins with optimization, a process that comprises three steps, which remain the same no matter which archetype is your primary. They are:

1. Recognize your primary archetype's strength and stress states.
2. Understand your primary archetype's individual needs for safety.
3. Achieve balance within your primary archetype.

As a result of optimizing your primary archetype, you will cultivate more empathy and compassion—for yourself and others—and replace old, ineffectual patterns with empowerment. You will embody stability and security in the face of upset. Optimization will also give you elegance and agility at times when you're feeling powerless or tossed about like a rudderless sailboat in response to unpredictable and unstable predicaments—and help you navigate those unchartered waters with more grace and stability.

Step One:
Recognizing Metal's Strength and Stress States

When your Metal archetype is balanced, you will notice that it contributes the strengths of beauty, organization, preparedness, and conscientiousness to your life, to your relationships, and to the broader community.

A balanced Metal also helps us:

+ Calm ourselves through the power of the breath.
+ Discriminate between what is good for us and what isn't.
+ Decide how to most effectively use our time.
+ Commit to a standard of moral values.
+ Have the patience to practice until we get something right.
+ Recognize quickly when things are out of place and need to be realigned.
+ Stay on time.
+ Remain focused for extended periods of time.
+ Learn from our mistakes.
+ Forgive ourselves and others.
+ Appreciate the gifts we have in the world.
+ Build and believe in our own self-worth.
+ Stay accountable to ourselves when we take on a project.
+ Perfect our skill before showing it to the world.
+ Connect with our higher purpose.
+ Keep our private life private.
+ Create consistent, reliable patterns of behavior.
+ Respect other people's boundaries.
+ Design with attention to detail.
+ Keep our physical space organized.
+ Remember important details.

We create symmetry and stability in our lives and in the lives of others when we have unfettered access to the positive aspects of our Metal archetype. But sometimes our Metal can become unstable and stressed and is not as available to us. When this happens, we don't feel clear or peaceful, and it's difficult to solve problems for ourselves or in our relationships. Luckily, Metal gives us warning signs to help us know when this is happening.

Stressed Metal manifests as:

+ Over-focusing on the details of a project.
+ Obsessing over the orderliness of your space.
+ Becoming too critical of yourself or others.
+ Feeling stuck in grief.
+ Too much blaming of other people and outside circumstances for your problems.
+ Getting stuck on things that happened in the past.
+ Compulsively cleaning or organizing.
+ Concerning yourself with trying to be perfect in every way.
+ Focusing so much on inequities and perceived wrongs that you can't see past little details and move forward with your ideas and initiatives.
+ Becoming easily annoyed or disappointed.
+ Feeling sad and not knowing why.
+ Living such a disciplined life that there's no room left for having fun.
+ Caring too much about being wrong or making mistakes.
+ Feeling emotionally unstable and withdrawn.
+ Experiencing discomfort as a result of a change in routine.
+ Having a hard time envisioning a positive future.
+ Caring so much about protecting people's boundaries that you avoid showing compassion and empathy.
+ Practicing too much.

At its core, recognizing your strong and stressed Metal characteristics in Step One is about shifting how you use your time. Many of us rush through life, hoping everything goes well and nothing gets in the way of our ticking off all the items on our to-do list. In such haste, we're more likely to ignore the early signs of internal stress and relationship problems. However, early detection allows us to stave off issues well before they become anxiety-provoking, painful challenges.

Step One in the optimization process invites you to make time to notice subtle clues that may direct you to course-correct, or perhaps stay right where you are and move a little faster toward your goal.

Start practicing this step by recognizing and tracking your Metal stress and strength states. Recognizing asks you to look and observe, not judge and criticize. Metal types tend to hold themselves to high standards and may find it challenging to accept that there is no right or wrong, good or bad inherent within their prospective stress and strength states. However, these states are your teachers. They help you know what type of action to take to ensure that you continue to strengthen your self-awareness and self-regulation skills as well as expand your healthy relationship skills. So the simple practice of noticing tendencies and motivations—such as how you feel when you choose to make eye contact with and smile at a stranger, or rather when you go out of your way not to do so—is an opportunity to identify where you are along your strength–stress spectrum and what you can do to move even closer to your strongest expression of yourself. Familiarize yourself with these lists, and remember to simply pay attention to your Metal tendencies.

Once you get used to noticing when and how your Metal states make themselves apparent in your daily life, you may also choose to track these symptoms or challenge states. Many people become pleasantly surprised at how easy it becomes to take more control over their challenging states and to self-regulate just by taking a moment to notice and chronicle their tendencies.

Over time, you may surprise yourself by spotting Metal patterns of thoughts and behaviors you usually miss when simply rushing through your day. When you slow down and take the time to notice your Metal states, you may become aware that your stressed thoughts and behaviors always reach an unpleasant peak around certain types of people in your life. You may notice that when your plans don't play out as expected, you tend to become more strict and overly critical of who may have "dropped the ball" when you never really realized you were so inclined before. You may also start to become cognizant of the fact that you're much more organized than others around you. As you become more sensitized to how your proclivities compare to those of others around you, you'll begin to develop a heightened sense of awareness for how your thoughts, behaviors, and belief systems impact them as well.

Step Two:
Understanding Metal's Needs for Safety

You now know how Metal takes form within you when it's strong and when it's stressed, but let's take a look at why primary Metals get stressed out in the first place.

As Dr. Cowan teaches in the Tournesol Kids #PowerUp program—a nonprofit we created together to teach parents, teachers, and kids the skills for self-awareness, self-regulation, and empathy—we only experience our stress states when our particular needs for safety are not met. Our individual needs for feeling secure correspond directly to our primary archetype. Just as Metal's strength and stress conditions are unique, so are the particular needs a primary Metal requires to feel balanced and avoid feeling too much stress.

For example, you'll see in the list below that primary Metal people require routine, structure, and consistency in their lives. When Metal people go too long without these needs being met, their stressed behaviors and feelings begin to manifest. However, it's up to them to recognize which needs are not being met and to make a plan to bring stability, precision, and calm back into their lives. If primary Metals were to expect others to meet their need for structure and discipline, they would be setting themselves up for disappointment, which leads to aggravation and criticism toward themselves and toward the people who "don't appreciate" them. Ultimately, expecting others to fulfill your needs for you only drives a wedge in your relationships and stokes emotions that make it difficult for you to access your gracious Metal gifts.

This is why I've created a "needs list" for primary Metals, inspired by what I've learned from Dr. Cowan, so you as an Architect can better understand your specific needs and avoid becoming stuck in antagonistic situations. Recognizing and meeting your individual needs for safety will help you feel strong, confident, and motivated to take risks that nurture yourself and your relationships.

NOTE: If Metal is not your primary archetype, you can still refer to this Metal's Needs List to better understand and empathize with the primary Metal people in your life. The more skilled you become at empathizing with the needs of others, the more success you'll have in your interpersonal relationships. For more information on how to more harmoniously interact with the other Metal types in your life, turn to page 221.

METAL'S NEEDS LIST

- Accuracy
- Adaptability
- Admiration
- Appreciation
- Assessment
- Attention
- Beauty
- Breathing
- Clarity
- Composure
- Consistency
- Continuity
- Cooperation
- Decorum
- Deference
- Devotion
- Dignity
- Discernment
- Esteem

- Familiarity
- Forgiveness
- Framework
- Grace
- Honesty
- Integrity
- Methods
- Meticulousness
- Morality
- Objectivity
- Opinion
- Perfection
- Polish
- Preciousness
- Predictability
- Preparation
- Procedure
- Proficiency
- Refinement

- Regard
- Respect
- Rhythm
- Righteousness
- Routine
- Schedule
- Self-control
- Self-worth
- Significance
- Specificity
- Stability
- Symmetry
- Systems
- Technique
- Tradition
- Training
- Understanding
- Value
- Virtue

If your primary archetype is Metal, use the needs list to help you:

- Feel relief more quickly in times of challenge.
- Feel less critical of yourself and others.
- Feel more motivated to figure out how to have your own needs met more of the time.

To help you get started, think of a current struggle you're having. Then take a look over the needs list to see if there is a need related to your struggle that you wish you could fulfill right now.

Be mindful that this needs exercise is not about what others aren't giving you or doing for you, as Dr. Cowan teaches. Instead, it's about gaining an awareness of which of your core needs for safety are not being met at that moment and figuring out what *you* can do to have them met.

Keep in mind that your individual "needs" work is about empowering yourself to observe how you're feeling and to take control over creating your own internal harmony. It's about figuring out how you can get your own needs met, not about expecting other people or outside circumstances to change so that you get what you want. I'd be willing to bet you've tried that before and have come up empty-handed. Expecting others to complete us simply doesn't work—sorry, Jerry McGuire!

This is not to say we shouldn't empathize with and care for each other or meet each other's needs within relationships. The sign of a strong relationship is when we can have compassion for and meet each other's shared needs for safety. Take a look back over Neha Chawla's advice for building and nurturing strong relationships on pages 36–38 for a refresher.

Remember that the only thing in this world you can control is you. Take some time to review the needs list that corresponds to your primary archetype. When your stress states creep up, pause instead of reacting. Then practice taking action to acquire the items on the list you need in your life. Doing so will reduce the frequency and severity of your stress states and allow you to recover from them more quickly and easily. As a result, you'll feel satisfied more of the time and enjoy more fulfilling relationships.

The highest level of having your needs met is being able to meet them for yourself. Being aware of and figuring out how to meet your needs for safety is the way to continuously grow stronger throughout your lifetime. When you're self-aware, self-reliant, empathetic, and empowered to meet your own needs, your life experience is exponentially elevated.

Step Two in the optimization process asks that you recognize which of your specific unmet Metal needs for safety are kicking up your uncomfortable emotions. The more you practice merely paying attention to your stress and strength states, the easier it will be for you to identify and even predict why you're feeling low. Making this connection subsequently brings you closer to taking control over the seemingly inexplicable ebb and flow of your emotions.

For example, Metal people are commonly triggered by things not going according to a preexisting or predefined plan. When Metal people know what to expect from the people around them, they have a better chance of avoiding messy, chaotic feelings and circumstances. Chaos provokes the Metal fear of things going wrong or mistakes being made. Faced with disorganized, muddled situations, Metal people have a tendency to become inflexible, and in extreme states—perhaps having had insufficient sleep and not enough time to eat—Metals can even feel grief-stricken.

Left unaddressed, these challenging emotions escalate. For Metal types, this could result in:

+ Becoming numb to your stress triggers.
+ Stiffening muscles.
+ Becoming overly strict and critical of yourself and those around you.

To start practicing Step Two as a primary Metal, examine a current stressor that's bothering you. Next, identify the feelings that come up for you as a result of this particular challenge. Your emotions are your need identifiers. Metal types sometimes react to the experience of feeling intense emotions by becoming disappointed in themselves or others. However, I'm asking you to pause with these uncomfortable emotions and instead of reacting, consider that your emotions are there to help you identify your unmet needs for safety in this moment. Once you've identified your feelings, pause and ask yourself what unmet need(s) the emotions are telling you that you should focus on from your needs list.

If you're feeling compulsive, disappointed, annoyed, or sad, Step Two asks you to notice it. Observe and don't react. Try to identify what your disillusioned Metal feelings are telling you that you need in that moment. Are you feeling unappreciated? Are your coworkers not adhering to company policy for projects you're working on together? Are people around you running late or being too pushy, silly, or overly naive?

Any of these examples can trigger uncomfortable emotions for primary Metal people, but the more you practice pausing and observing what comes up for you when you feel unpleasant emotions, the more you'll remain calm and realize which of your needs aren't being met instead of experiencing frustration and self-critical thinking. Once you know your stress triggers, you have more power to prevent their negative impact.

Step Three:
Achieving Balance Within the Metal Archetype

Step Three in the optimization process is about taking action. This is the step for building your foundation of resilience and making new stress-response choices. This is where you begin to build new habits and behaviors, which translate into the creation of new and healthier neural pathways over time and, ultimately, balance within your primary archetype.

Armed with new information about the source of your stressors from Step Two, you're more aware of where your unpleasant feelings are coming from. You understand that they're directly related to whether or not you're having your needs for safety met. Other people and outside circumstances may initiate uncomfortable events, but how you choose to respond is ultimately your decision. If you elect to react while your Metal is unbalanced, you and those around you will spend more time in discomfort.

On the other hand, if your Metal is balanced, you will be more in control of your reactive states under stress and actually reduce the amount of time you and the others spend upset. Reducing your reactivity enables clarity of thought, creativity, smooth conflict resolution, and unconditional love. When you have more control over your stress reactions, you will live a more fulfilling and well-adjusted life.

Let's get to the core of how to cultivate a balanced Metal archetype. While Metal is the power of creating rightness, routine, and predictability in relationships, if Metal is not nurtured and contained properly, it can distort your ability to feel balanced and strong. The Metal archetype needs to support you by contributing its graciousness instead of its overly rigid perceptions and opinions. You also need Metal's strengths to be balanced so they help calm, temper, and balance the stress states of the other types within you. Ultimately, as a primary Metal, your Metal archetype needs to work for you so it can improve your life, instead of making it stressful.

Your Metal-Balancing Skills

Balanced Metal presents itself as the ability to live honorably and have the emotional flexibility to both inspire others to recognize and choose a moral path as well as to gently forgive those who are still on the road to developing their personal sense of discernment.

As you know, in its most balanced state, Metal is guided by the desire to create and hold space for graceful consistency and shared ideals, helping support and shape the relationships and organizations they value. But just as metal that is too inflexible or too malleable cannot provide proper protection and reinforcement, Metal's instability can manifest as becoming too preoccupied with creating the perfect scenario; a Metal person can lose sight of the bigger picture or become so focused on following the rules that they don't notice when it's better for all if they create new, updated guidelines.

We become balanced by taking specific and consistent action that builds and protects the body, mind, and spirit components of our arche-typal nature. Eastern well-being philosophies like TCM state that whole health is not achieved by simply addressing one of these three aspects of our overall being. They teach that these aspects are inextricably connected within us. For example, a physical imbalance causes emotional unrest, which manifests as larger existential conundrums. Consummate balance is the result of a combined effort to empower all three intertwined parts. Thus, you'll notice that the tasks for balancing all five archetypes draw upon all three realms: mind, body, and spirit.

✦ ✦ ✦ ✦ ✦

Now that you're familiar with Steps One and Two of the optimization process, in which you learned about Metal's archetypal traits and needs for safety, it's time to learn how to balance your Metal archetype—and even how to help other Metal types do the same.

There are two important ways of doing so:

+ Self-care in the moment
+ Long-term maintenance

Metal Self-Care in the Moment

Metal self-care in a moment of heightened stress calls for different skills from those you'll build over time to bolster your resilience. Faced with a troublesome, bitter situation, a primary Metal person is going to be hard-pressed to avoid becoming over-focused on small details or becoming too critical of others. Under challenging circumstances, it becomes hard for Metal to envision ways to move past problems rather than thinking of every single thing that is going wrong. When Metals feel completely over-whelmed, they can't easily release their grip on needing the stressful situation to resolve the way *they* believe it should.

But in Metal's challenging moments, when one is feeling most stuck in the weeds on an issue, Water serves as Metal's immediate release valve. Water activities, behaviors, thoughts, and people are the most likely to help Metal rebalance and recover from a heightened state of stress.

Some Water tools for releasing the initial pressure include:

+ Pause and rest for a minute to counteract your need to take action right away. This gives your mind time to listen and gain more clarity about your needs and those of the people and circumstances around you.
+ Take a drink of room-temperature or warm water.
+ Listen to calming music.
+ Remember a time when you recovered well from something like this before.
+ Get quiet; close your eyes. Listen to and name five sounds you hear in the room.
+ Meditate for a few minutes on the colors silver, white, or blue.
+ Read something you enjoy that doesn't directly relate to the problem at hand.
+ Go for a slow, quiet walk alone around the block.
+ Spend a few minutes journaling about the details and emotions surrounding your stressful situation.

Once the severity of the emotions subsides, you'll regain the composure to mobilize skills from all five archetypes to help you resolve the problem that initiated the feelings of insecurity in the first place. When you, as a primary Metal, feel adequately calm and prepared to begin problem solving, choose the archetype-based activities from the lists on pages 216–20 that correspond to the strengths you most need in the moment. Examples of the strengths that correspond to each type are:

+ **Wood:** You'll need to engage your Wood skills if your problem requires you to widen your perspective and envision the overall arc of a plan or to take immediate action toward achieving your goal.

+ **Fire:** You'll need to draw upon your Fire skills if your problem requires easing off from your initial beliefs and assumptions about how things *should* be so that you can appreciate the various, unconventional opinions and feelings of other people.

+ **Earth:** You'll need to access your Earth skills if your issue requires trusting other people, collaboration, teaching skills, or finding out and meeting everyone else's wants and needs.

+ **Metal:** You'll want to dip into your Metal skills if one of the causes of your problem is that there is not enough structure for things to run smoothly and predictably.

+ **Water:** You'll reach for your Water skills if your issue requires more time to think things through, a more thorough evaluation of all the components impacting your challenge, or sitting back and really listening to everyone's concerns without judgment.

Metal Long-Term Maintenance

Another way to achieve balance in your Metal archetype is to practice your maintenance activities over the long term to help ensure you remain resilient in the face of stress as you progress. With a stable, reliable foundation of resilience built up, you're better prepared to observe life's challenges rather than react to them. The more advanced you become at avoiding reactive states, the more quickly you will recover from stress states and return to enjoying life.

Begin your maintenance regimen by practicing activities that support your primary Metal archetype. Start by choosing one or two activities from the Metal list to practice every day.

Next, identify one or two activities from the archetype list that correspond to the archetype in which you scored the lowest. Add these items to your daily Metal archetype routine. Don't forget, it's important to practice your lowest archetype, even if it's your least favorite type of activity (which I'm willing to bet it is). Exercising your most vulnerable archetype minimizes the gap between your highest and lowest archetypes, expanding your ability to be more emotionally dexterous when challenges arise.

Finally, practice activities that correlate to the challenges you're currently facing. Here are some examples to help you identify which archetypal skills in the lists on pages 50–59 you will need and will find most helpful as a primary Metal:

- If you're having trouble make a big decision and taking action to implement it, add in some Wood-building activities.
- If you want to improve your ability to listen to other people's opinions, empower your skills for getting quiet, and hear what everyone else notices about a particular challenge, work on your Water abilities.
- If you're not feeling compelled to share and collaborate in meetings, focus on expanding your Earth skills to build more tolerance and appreciation for the benefits of teamwork and cooperation.
- If you find yourself spending too much time pointing out problems and inconsistencies, practice some Fire activities to expand your ability to consider things from an optimistic perspective.

Choose from among these Metal activities to get you started on building your Metal maintenance regimen:

+ Create some structure within your day and do your best to stick to it—whether it's a morning routine, eating meals around the same time each day, creating a bedtime routine or maintaining a routine for prayer or worship. Come up with a process for measuring your success in keeping up with your routines.

+ Observe negative thoughts that arise about yourself, others, and situations. Notice them, and then see if you can practice letting them go with a firm exhale through your mouth.

+ Pay attention to the times you don't feel forgiving toward yourself or others—just observe, and don't judge yourself for it.

+ Recognize when you're focusing on the same details for prolonged periods of time.

+ Practice making small, inconsequential mistakes, such as leaving something out of place on the dining room table when you go to sleep at night, to expand your ability to tolerate mishaps.

+ Adopt a breathwork practice that you like and do it regularly.

+ Upon waking and right before you fall asleep at night, think of three people for whom you're grateful. Alternately, start a gratitude practice once per day to focus on things and people in your life for whom you're appreciative. List the specific reasons why you're grateful.

+ Track your stress triggers and patterns so you can have more control over them in the future.
+ Participate in self-care that gives you personalized attention, like acupuncture or Ayurveda.
+ Metal corresponds to the sense of smell. Use aromatherapy at home and at work if appropriate. Aromas that support balanced Metal include:

+ Myrrh	+ Bergamot	+ Lavender
+ Chamomile	+ Blue chamomile	+ Lemon
+ Linden blossom	+ Frankincense	
+ Benzoin	+ Hyssop	

+ Choose or create your own ritual, one that means something to you, and practice it regularly.
+ Practice something that requires coordination and focus to get better, like playing a musical instrument or creating a painting or sculpture.
+ Attend regular services at a religious or spiritual house of worship.

Earth-Building Activities

+ Become part of a community of kind, trustworthy people whom you see regularly.
+ Volunteer at a nonprofit whose mission aligns with your personal calling.
+ Make sure you're eating well and that you have healthy digestion. Pay attention to the relationship your body has with your food. Notice whether you feel constipated, gassy, or bloated, or if you have acid reflux. If

your digestion feels shaky, seek the guidance of a nutrition specialist to get it back on track.

+ Find one item or meal to eat mindfully each day, appreciating every bite, chewing slowly, and pausing between bites. Consider trying to chew twenty times per bite.

+ Consider joining a class that teaches or practices a group-based activity like dancing, singing, or cooking.

+ Make time to talk regularly with someone you trust who can help you gain perspective when you feel stuck.

+ Make a point of building a compassionate rapport with people you see regularly. Remember their names and details about their lives, and inquire about them to show you care.

Water-Building Activities

+ Make sure you're drinking enough water each day.

+ Massage your hands and feet with a little coconut oil before bed each night.

+ Journal, reflecting on your day, thoughts, feelings, and relationships.

+ Listen to gentle, calming music.

+ Read a book you enjoy.

+ Learn a meditation practice that suits you and meditate at the same time each day. Your Metal will appreciate the structure.

+ Take a bath with Epsom salts and lavender oil, or another scent that appeals to you.

+ Go swimming.

+ Take a slow walk in nature, preferably near a body of water.

- Try to get to bed before midnight—as close to 10:00 p.m. as possible.
- Rest quietly for a few minutes with one hand over your heart and the other over your abdomen.
- Play memory games.
- Feng shui your home or office.

Wood-Building Activities

- Take some time to schedule out your plans for the upcoming days. This can be anything from planning your shopping for the daily family dinner menu to scheduling some quiet time for yourself. Make some time to review and solidify your long-term plans as well.
- Create a regular exercise routine that meets your specific physical needs. Consider working with a trainer to learn the best strategy for your body type and strength level. Consider incorporating practices that combine breathing with stretching and moving, like yoga, qi gong, or tai chi.
- Surround yourself with soothing colors that reflect nature, like greens, blues, and tans.
- Spend time outside. Take a walk. Lie down in the grass. Literally change your perspective, and watch how nature goes with the flow, not against it.
- Cultivate a home garden or plants in your space.
- Imagine how you'll feel after specific, bothersome situations are resolved.
- Do some head rolls and yoga neck stretches to loosen up the throat area.

Fire-Building Activities

+ Schedule time to engage in fun activities with friends.
+ Practice articulating your emotions, which is a self-nurturing way to deal with feeling stuck and unsettled. Recognize and say how you feel—first to yourself and then to those around you when you develop the courage to do so. Over time, when you're entwined in a conflict, you'll become less easily stuck in unpleasant emotions, and you'll start to remember that things will get better.
+ Smile at yourself in the mirror. Some studies show that your body can't produce the stress hormone cortisol when you're smiling.
+ Practice heart-opening yoga stretches like cat/cow and cobra.
+ Identify your mixed emotions in times of calm and in times of frustration, without judging them; just observe them.

Ultimately, your Metal archetype is balanced when you:

+ Have easier, more regular access to—and pay attention to—your sense of your own intuition.
+ Anticipate and feel more consistently excited about future plans, activities, and projects.
+ Look more forward to travel and adventure.
+ Spend less time being hyperaware of your own or others' mistakes.
+ Notice more easily when you judge yourself for having emotions you believe you shouldn't.

+ Have strong digestion more of the time.
+ Empathetically reach out to others more, inquiring about their well-being and how you can support them.
+ Are less resistant to evaluating how you may have contributed to an interpersonal challenge.
+ Are more open to trying new restaurants, new clothing brands, and new ways of doing things.
+ Laugh and relax more easily in social situations.
+ Are more consciously aware of your strength and stress states.
+ Enjoy spending more time outside.
+ Have more balanced moods.
+ Know your needs for safety.
+ Are able to have your needs met and to self-regulate with ease in times of stress.

Harmonization

I don't want to leave you hanging, wondering when and how you'll know you're in harmony as a primary Metal.

Again, harmonization is not an absence of stress and challenge. For primary Metals, it's about being able to navigate the challenging moments of your own life while empathizing with and supporting those around you whose Metal archetype may be low and in need of a boost. At its core, harmonization allows you to have unconditional love for yourself and those around you.

When you, as a primary Metal, are harmonized, you're likely to experience many, if not all, of the attitudes and behaviors noted below.

+ You consistently notice, honor, and can clearly see and take control of the connections

- between the amount and quality of time spent with friends and family and how much you restrict or hold back sharing your feelings in relationships.
- between the cadence of your breath and the amount of inflexibility you experience.
- between the amount of good sleep you get and how much you obsess over small details, or how much sadness and grief you feel.
- between how regularly you exercise and how much more you accomplish in a day.
- between how often you acknowledge your emotions without judging them and how much more easily you experience a sense of joy and optimism.

- You are comfortable "coloring outside the lines."
- You appreciate exploring the things in life you're passionate about for the sake of personal enjoyment.
- You spend time taking care of others, even when it's not what you had planned to do.
- You seek out opportunities to be alone with your thoughts, a book, or journaling.
- You experiment with letting others decide the "rules of engagement."
- You ask others what they think about how a project should be done.
- You don't feel the need to blame others, but instead take time to gather information and learn how to help the entire group be more effective next time.
- You are able to plan and even have a backup plan for getting things done, understanding that it's okay if things don't go right the first time.
- You are less baffled when people don't keep their word.

+ You don't feel the need to determine the standards of behavior in a relationship.
+ You can recognize grief coming on and can ease your way out of it on your own more easily.

METAL IN RELATIONSHIPS

As our personal awareness and resilience in the face of stress expands, we are less triggered by other people's moods, opinions, and tendencies. We also become less likely to attach to relationships that don't serve us well or in which our needs for safety aren't being met. As we strengthen our individual Five Archetypes skills, we are better equipped to form equally strong bonds with individuals from any one of the Five Archetypes because we see the benefit and the beauty of the gifts they each bring to the companionship.

In this section, primary Metal will gain guidance for building and maintaining propitious relationships, and non-primary Metals will learn how to engage in healthy relationships with primary Metal types.

If You Are a Metal/Architect

To be a good Metal partner in any relationship, practice staying in balance by knowing your strengths, challenges, and needs, and by practicing the Metal long-term maintenance activities starting on page 216 to remain a consistently stable partner. This will ensure you approach relationship challenges from a place of calm compassion for yourself and your companions.

When you commit to doing the work that keeps your Metal in balance, you contribute the following strengths to your interpersonal relationships:

- Exercising discretion in keeping your secrets secret.
- Organizing a balanced social and work life as a couple.
- Making sure to meet each other's expectations and not repeating mistakes that negatively impact the relationship in the future.
- Not allowing a bad mood to impact the relationship.
- Keeping a partner, kids, or colleagues from engaging in unsafe situations.
- Articulating details of how you see a problem and the process for solving it.
- Maintaining steadfast focus on the needs of the relationship without becoming distracted by outside influences.
- Keeping an organized home so the whole family benefits from the clarity you experience from living within a contained, structured environment: "uncluttered space = uncluttered mind."
- Avoiding intensity, preferring a calm and even-keeled relationship.
- Creating a predictable home life so everyone feels safe and knows what to expect.
- Consistently treating a partner with respect.
- Noticing unhealthy patterns in the relationship that need attention so they can be improved upon.

When your primary Metal is balanced, you also possess the following characteristics that benefit the global community:

- Knowing from experience what is needed to improve the state of the community.
- Making sure everything happens on time, as expected.
- Upholding righteous standards.

+ Giving clear and coherent instructions for how to organize an effort to make the most effective impact.
+ Behaving in a respectful manner, earning the admiration of followers far and wide.
+ Creating an organized effort from everyone's visions, creative ideas, thoughts, and dreams.
+ Knowing from past experience what is going to work well and what won't.
+ Figuring out how best to implement big plans.
+ Defining the specific steps needed for a project to be fully successful.
+ Serving as a moral leader and determining the most honorable efforts for creating a better world and life experience for the masses.
+ Analyzing the most efficacious way forward by evaluating what has worked in the past.
+ Setting up methods for measuring progress to make sure the organization is achieving desired goals in a timely manner.
+ Making sure the team doesn't act too hastily for the initiative to be fully realized, successful, and sustainable.

On the other hand, when your primary Metal is not balanced, it shows up in your interpersonal relationships as:

+ Creating unrealistic expectations of your partner and holding them accountable.
+ Cutting people off when they don't meet standards you create for both of you.
+ Judging your partner's words and actions instead of listening openly to what their actions say about their unmet needs for safety within the relationship.

+ Becoming stuck grieving over things your partner did in the past and not being able to forgive or move forward.
+ Requiring unflinching perfection from your partner.
+ Over-focusing on inequities and perceived wrongs.
+ Becoming easily annoyed or disappointed by your partner.
+ Seeing too much value in being the sole authority, and leaving no room for others to develop their leadership skills.
+ Believing so strongly in principled behavior that there's no room for flexibility and spontaneity.
+ Believing you're always right and your partner is always wrong.
+ Preferring being right to being in a relationship.
+ Becoming cold and reserving passion in the face of a relationship conflict as a punishment for your partner.
+ Liking things to stay the same, and worrying if the relationship shifts and changes.
+ Taking things too literally, and missing the subtle meaning behind words and in body language.
+ Focusing only on the negative, and struggling to see the good in your partner or in the relationship.
+ Holding back too much and not feeling safe enough to share deep emotions.

When your primary Metal is unbalanced, watch out for these potential behaviors that could manifest and affect your global community:

+ Can't easily access your instinctive ability to know the next steps required to move a project forward.
+ Over-caring about making sure everything and everyone adheres to a strict timeline.

+ Not being able to tell when creating and upholding righteous standards for the group becomes self-righteousness and is no longer truly virtuous.
+ Giving instructions that serve yourself more than the greater purpose.
+ Judging past behaviors and experiences instead of being able to analyze and take away the most important lessons learned to improve processes going forward.
+ Becoming so over-concerned with details that you hold the project back from being rolled out in a timely manner.
+ Believing there's only one right way to execute a successful plan.
+ Becoming so picky hiring the right people for positions that you end up missing out on candidates who could grow into the position and bring fresh ideas to a concept.

If You Have a Relationship with a Metal/Architect

In the following pages, you will learn how primary Metals exhibit themselves at work, in intimate relationships, and as parents. Remember, *The Five Archetypes* is a primer for beginners, so I'm just touching on the basic concepts to help you understand, evaluate, and adjust the flow of the primary Metal archetype within you for the best personal and interpersonal outcomes.

The Metal Employee or Coworker

When applied to the workplace, the Five Archetypes method expands your ability and the ability of your coworkers to get things done efficiently. Moreover, when employees and colleagues feel safe, seen, understood, and appreciated in the workplace, they navigate challenges more easily and therefore are less reactive when in stress states, which ultimately translates to a healthier bottom line.

To enhance your awareness of times when your Metal staff or coworkers feel safe and when they feel insecure, there are some common tendencies to watch out for. When you see your colleagues exhibiting their insecure states, it's time to pause and fortify yourself so you don't jump into your reactive states as a result. Get to know these common strengths, needs, and stress states:

- Strengths at Work: Metal staff are terrific at creating beauty, paying attention to important details, and designing with perfection. They respect authority and have excellent analytical skills.
- Needs at Work: Metal needs clearly defined job responsibilities and supervisory expectations. This allows them to autonomously measure their success. It's also important to Metal that meetings begin and end on time.
- Potential Challenges and Stress States: Stressed Metals have a tendency to feel quite hurt when archetypal needs aren't met at work and disconcerted when others don't follow the rules. Metals may get so overfocused on getting the small details right that they unnecessarily keep projects from moving forward in a timely manner.
- Here's how to nurture Metal employees over time and how to help them release stress in the moment.
  - Support in the Moment: Redirect your stressed Metal employee or coworker to take a step back from the details in which he or she is getting caught up. Encourage the Metal person to rest, take some

time away from the project, and listen to some soothing music. The space away from the challenge helps them move forward more easily with their project by reducing their tendency to become too stuck on the details or on what's not working.

+ Ongoing Encouragement: Nurture a sense of high-quality design, structure, and continuity over time with your Metal employee or colleague through structured and regular staff and/or one-on-one meetings, where they can participate in sharing ideas, get feedback, and feel appreciated as a part of the bigger picture in a safe, supportive environment.

The Metal Friend

Enjoying mutually gratifying friendships starts with *you* knowing how to be a good friend to others. To consistently show up as a steady, sincere, reliable friend, check out these Five Archetypes guidelines:

+ Learn your primary archetype strengths, challenges, and needs so you can practice becoming and staying self-aware.
+ Make sure your need for safety is being met within the relationship.
ı Recognize and take responsibility for your reactive states, and practice your self-regulation techniques.
+ Adopt a mind-set in which you see challenge as an invitation to grow, not an excuse to judge or criticize others.
+ Discover your friends' needs for safety so you can practice compassionate consideration.

How Do We Nurture Lasting Friendships?

As a friendship grows, how do we continue to nurture and strengthen our bond using the Five Archetypes method? When you know your friend's primary archetype, you will better understand what makes them feel safe and what makes them feel insecure. Here are some additional suggestions for what primary Metal people will likely appreciate in a close friendship.

Metals like spending time with people who:

+ Share similar life values.
+ Can appreciate the beauty in details with them, either in home decorating or at a fine arts museum.
+ Enjoy having a regular get-together date and value being on time.
+ Like activities such as craft-making or cooking classes.

Helping a Metal Friend in Stress

When you care about someone, you sympathize with their pain and want them to feel better. The Five Archetypes model helps us understand that people have unique stress triggers as well as different paths to de-stressing. Here's how to help your primary Metal friends recover more quickly from stress states.

Encourage a Metal friend out of stress states by complimenting their efforts as ingenious, significant, sharp, and original. Metals will also feel better when accompanying you to a structured group activity like yoga, jewelry making, or pottery.

The Metal Romantic Partner

Primary Metal people in their balanced state contribute a sense of reliability to a relationship. Your Metal partner will always show up on time and build a stable home in which you can both flourish. She doesn't get too drawn into emotional reactions; rather, she's rational and appreciates the higher purpose of all your efforts as a couple. She creates continuity and organization in your day-to-day life, so your mind is less cluttered and more able to handle all the more complicated situations. She's deeply grateful for everything you do and notices even your subtle efforts. She gently teaches wisdom begotten from her own hard-earned life lessons and forgives you during your growing pains and learning processes.

When Metal types feel insecure, they exhibit specific patterns of disharmony in a relationship. Stressed Metals fear being wrong and may hold on to the need to be right over the need to be in love (you know, the whole "see the forest for the trees" thing). When they feel insecure, Metals may get stuck on the past or on details of what their partner did instead of looking forward to a potentially better future.

Here are some tips for how you can be a strong partner to a primary Metal type.

- Do: Show up on time and let her know how much you appreciate who she is and what she contributes to your life.
- Don't: Forget about commitments you've made to her or laugh at her attempts to show respect and honor important moments.
- Help Her Refocus in Stress: Show your appreciation and tell her how much it meant to you when she went out of her way to create a well-organized evening, event, or space.
- Best Form of Consistent Encouragement: Invite your Metal partner to take part in regular group exercises or activities with you. She'll enjoy the opportunity to improve on or learn a new skill and feel cared for, honored, and included.

The Parent–Metal Child Relationship

Your parent-child relationship is impacted not only by the intersection between your and your child's primary archetypes but also by how you perceive your purpose as a parent. When you see your parental role as compassionate guide and teacher and empower your kids to master life skills so they become strong, resilient adults, you're more likely to build a strong relationship with your child and feel fulfilled by the parenting journey.

To create a gratifying relationship with your primary Metal child using the Five Archetypes method, start by identifying and balancing your own primary archetype. Get to know yourself in strength and in stress. Understand your button pushers so that you're best able to remain in a state of resilience and compassionate power when faced with your triggers. You'll be the most outstanding advocate and nurture a respectful, strong relationship with your child when you serve as a heroic example of how to manage stress, triggers, and disappointment.

Then, find out your child's primary archetype. Help her become more self-aware and self-reliant by teaching her how to recognize and celebrate her gifts. Empower her to overcome stress states with ease by helping her understand what pushes her buttons and giving her the Five Archetypes tools to become more resilient to her triggers.

Dr. Cowan is a pioneer of using the five types as a methodology for healthy child development. Here are some points, inspired by his work, to keep in mind when parenting a child whose primary archetype is Metal:

- Learning style: Metal kids learn by practicing.
- Sleeping: Metal kids are drawn to ritual and traditional practices before going to bed. Whether your custom is evening prayer, meditation, or something completely unique to your family, Metal kids enjoy this special and sacred time.

+ Eating: Metal kids like to eat the proper food, in the proper amounts, and at the proper time. Don't be surprised if your Metal child is the one who doesn't like any two foods on her plate to touch.
+ Exercise: Metal kids are motivated to learn the right way to practice the exercise that's best for them. They like a regular routine, and they like to practice improving their skill and ability.
+ Feelings: Metal kids don't always have an easy time expressing their emotions. They may judge their feelings, thinking they shouldn't be feeling anger, fear, or anxiety. It's important for them to practice naming their feelings without judgment so they know that feelings are okay.

METAL AYURVEDIC PRACTICES

Metal people are keen to identify the wellness practices that are the best for helping them achieve their goals. Once they identify the right practices, Metals tend to stay the course, preferring a regular routine over trying a variety of different approaches. For example, Metal people will likely ask around for the top personal trainer in the area, trusting that they have the most experience, best training, and strongest reputation and will provide the most valuable and accurate advice. Whichever path they choose, Metal people do well with regular exercise since it helps their body and mind remain flexible.

If you're a primary Metal, find someone who can give you detailed instructions for how to get the most out of your wellness activities. Round out your pursuits with guidance on nutrition, meditation, and breathwork as well.

With regard to incorporating Ayurvedic wellness practices into your everyday life, remember that the Metal archetype corresponds to the fifth Chakra. In the chart on the next page, you will find some gentle Ayurvedic practices that will help engage and balance this chakra.

The fifth Chakra is known as the Throat Chakra. According to Ayurveda, the Throat Chakra governs the power of the spoken word and the expression of fearless, authentic truth. The fifth Chakra correlates to the Metal archetype in a few ways. Metal corresponds to the physical component of the breath, which originates through the Throat Chakra. They both correlate to truth, refinement, and hidden feelings and emotions.

Using Ayurvedic practices is a safe and empowering option to complement any health-care or wellness regimen. Peruse the selection of Ayurvedic lifestyle practices below that correspond to your primary Metal archetype. Feel free to try the ones that feel like a good fit as you assemble your menu of healthy lifestyle activities.

Fifth Chakra—Throat

Oversees: This chakra is the center for sound, communication, speech, writing, thought expression

Location: Throat, ears, thyroid, parathyroid, neck, jaw, vocal cords

Color: Blue

Mantra: Ham

Yoga: Cat/cow with lion's breath, plow pose, shoulder stand, fish pose, baby cobra pose, legs up the wall pose

Gemstones: Aquamarine, turquoise

Mudra (a hand gesture that's said to stimulate a specific sense of focus and balance): Acceptance mudra, bhudy mudra

Foot marma (a pressure point that's said to enhance mind-body balance when massaged): Point below the pinky toe and at the outside edge of the foot

Aromatherapy: Chamomile, linden blossom, myrrh, benzoin, bergamot, blue chamomile, frankincense, hyssop, lavender, lemon

Taste: Bitter

A Final Note to Primary Metals

Dear Metal Friends,

As you discern new ways to incorporate the Five Archetypes into your daily routines, I'd like to leave you with some words of guidance and thanks.

Remember, your need for justice and precision can sometimes hamper your desire for emotionally fulfilling and significant relationships. Experiment with what it feels like to allow critical thoughts to appear and then let them go, taking small steps toward more flexibility in your social interactions. You may find that you enjoy the new diversity you invite into your life.

You are the epitome of integrity. I'm amazed by your unmatched ability to see the hand of a higher power in otherwise mundane or emotionally difficult situations. I am indebted to you for:

+ *Providing the structure that helps me remain productive every day and not get too lost chasing what I find fun in the moment.*
+ *Helping me edit and edit and edit and re-edit this book.*
+ *Reminding me that there is virtue in washing all the dishes and not leaving a few for the next day because I got bored with the monotony of cleaning up.*

I wrote a haiku for you in honor of the gifts you bestow upon the world.

> *Architect of style*
> *You remind us what is right*
> *Always keep your cool*

> *With gratitude,*
> *Carey*

WATER

THE PHILOSOPHER

I f you scored highest in Water traits on your assessment and have confirmed that your results are accurate, then Water is your primary archetype.

When Water is your primary archetype, its even, steady insight directs the way you interact with your environment. You share the gifts of knowledge, enlightenment, contentment, and courage with the world.

Water reveals itself in the simple delight of an afternoon spent basking in the beauty of nature, reflecting on the wonder of our delicate and brilliant ecosystem. Water is a deep and dreamy night's sleep that fortifies your overworked mind and body. It's the complete intoxication of escaping into the fantasy world of a Tolkien novel and reading all night, impervious to the passing of time and surprised by the rising of the morning sun. Water is the fortitude to see clearly through the mess of muddled emotions, worries, and time constraints of others so you can deftly and imaginatively solve complex problems.

Primary Water types are skeptics. They're never gullible, nor do they simply accept your optimistic instincts. They want to know the motivations behind your professions of love because they do not take compliments or promises at face value. They evaluate options thoroughly and don't hastily jump into business deals or relationships. They know deep in their soul that good things come to those who wait.

The "wise, trustworthy" friend, Water is adept at saving you from a convoluted, messy situation. Teaching us that there is deep value in pausing with our emotions instead of reacting to them is profoundly satisfying for Water types. Serving as a wise sage inculcates in them a lasting sense of self-worth.

The Water archetype, also known as "The Philosopher," is associated with deep, immersive thought, insight, and a desire for solitude. On the flip side, Water's typical lifestyle challenges include making sure to stay connected to their social network and avoiding the tendency to over-isolate or become too pessimistic. Primary Waters also struggle to overcome the fear of becoming obsolete or unable to contribute anything of meaning.

If Water is not your primary archetype, you will still have some amount of Water in your nature, so in order to achieve and maintain harmony throughout your lifetime, it's essential that you know where your Water ranks with respect to the other four archetypes and practice the skills that help keep the Water in your nature balanced. The long-term maintenance practices beginning on page 258 will help you both optimize your primary archetype and harmonize overall, as well as build a firm foundation of resilience in the face of stress. If Water is your primary, practicing your long-term maintenance activities will naturally propel you to recover from feelings of fear in times of stress and will increase your ability to access your strong introspection and objectivity skills. If Water is your lowest, practicing these activities will slow down obsessive worry and panic and will empower you to nurture ideas over time and appreciate the process rather than rushing through to finish projects and initiatives.

When Water Is Your Primary Archetype

If Water is your primary or is tied as one of your two primaries, this chapter applies most directly to you and how you understand and engage in your relationships.

As a primary Water, your courageous quest for truth is unparalleled. You have vast imaginative capabilities and radiate a wise, peaceful disposition to those around you. When you're feeling empowered, your friends, family, and community regard you as a gentle sage who is a focused listener and an outstanding problem solver. However, when you don't feel safe within your environment and you're not at your best, you feel alone and misunderstood, questioning your abilities and retreating from the world. In these low moments, it becomes difficult to access your natural, impressive talents.

Primary Water types live their highest spiritual purpose by tranquilly perceiving and sharing the deeper meanings of life, from regular everyday interactions to the greater significance of why we're here. They serve as our patient, peaceful guides, people we seek out for advice and direction. Waters living their most harmonious lives demonstrate to the world that we don't have to get caught up in heightened emotions or worry much about our inner critics. They show us how to calmly reflect on challenging situations, perceiving new ways forward that our high levels of distress and anxiety tend to obscure. As a result of their efforts, primary Waters hope that others begin to model this peaceful seeking of answers and new possibilities by mimicking Water's natural skills.

Primary Water types who feel confident and secure in who they are will embody distinct traits in their physical, mental, and spiritual being. Physically, Water types get good rest and maintain healthy sleep habits.

Mentally, Water types are incredible listeners and problem solvers who don't feel the need to rush to a conclusion just for the sake of speed. On the contrary, they appreciate taking the time to immerse themselves in issues and information to make sure they arrive at the wisest decision. Spiritually, primary Water types embody and share the gift of peace, demonstrating that even in the face of conflict, we can pause our racing thoughts, find quiet within ourselves, and create an effective outcome.

When your primary archetype is Water, you'll exhibit distinguishing capabilities and attitudes. These qualities persist and are expressed regularly in your personal behaviors and preferences, the self-care activities you favor, and the way others perceive you.

Here are a couple of basic Water archetype indicators to be aware of: When feeling resilient, primary Water people solve complex problems with ease, avoiding the trap of becoming entangled in other people's emotions and ensnared in human drama. On the other hand, when feeling insecure, Water types lack their usual sense of tenacity and willpower, retreating into their inner thoughts and believing they don't have anything of value to add.

This is why it's important for Waters to recognize when it's time to self-regulate, rather than react in a maladaptive manner when faced with challenge. Sometimes we become so caught up in our dysfunctional thoughts and belief patterns that we can't easily distinguish between rightful action and reactive behavior. To help you know when you're in a state of imbalance and are more likely to make a dysfunctional choice, Water types should be on the lookout for times when they:

+ Feel adrift and too distracted to focus on the present, so they lose track of time or misplace things.
+ Believe that nobody understands them.
+ Become so apprehensive about their own wisdom that they disengage and stop trying.

The ultimate outcomes I hope you achieve as a result of practicing the Five Archetypes method as a primary Water are twofold: self-empowerment and empathy for others. I want you to strengthen your personal resolve. I want you to know your unique brand of Water-centered resilience so you can exercise it in the face of friction and conflict. When life's influences and forces lead you toward choices and behaviors that feel most Water-type comfortable, such as over-isolating in times of stress, I want you to have the awareness to recognize that your comfort zone is not always your sacred path. With time and patience, you'll establish a foundation of insight and understanding for how to maintain your individuality while simultaneously enveloping those around you with compassion and kindness.

When Water Is Your Secondary Archetype

If Water is your secondary archetype, it modifies your primary way of engaging in the world, meaning Water behaviors and proclivities more often reveal themselves within your character than your lower three archetypal traits, but not as often as your primary traits.

For instance, as a secondary Water, you may notice that Water-specific challenges such as not having enough time to think through problems can irk you. These Water-typical challenges won't chronically provoke you the way your primary trials will, but you will likely notice times when you have Water needs you want met and Water frustrations you seek to avoid. Arm yourself with the Water knowledge in this chapter so you have access to Water-balancing activities when the need arises.

Here are some archetype-based traits you may notice in yourself or others who have secondary Water:

+ Metal people with secondary Water will have an easier time letting go of overcritical and rigid thoughts by reflecting, listening, and adopting a broader perspective on challenges.

+ Wood people with secondary Water will be more likely to take the extra time to carefully reflect upon the possible positive outcomes and problematic pitfalls of a new idea before launching it into the world.
+ Fire people with secondary Water will not be quite as gullible when receiving compliments or when evaluating the benefits of potential new opportunities. Instead, Fire will likely take compliments with a grain of salt and spend time assessing both the advantages and shortcomings of new connections and projects.
+ Earth people with secondary Water will want very much to become involved in your life, but will appreciate some quiet alone time to recover from a lot of interpersonal engagement, and they're less likely to ruminate very long about whether or not they fit in with the crowd.

When Water Is Your Lowest Archetype

Becoming aware of the fact that Water is your lowest archetype sheds light on the archetype-based skills that may be harder for you to access overall. Your low Water is likely to become more evident to you in times of stress when you can't quiet your worry or panicked thoughts.

If Water is your lowest archetype, you may not be drinking enough water or getting good sleep. You may also struggle creating adequate time to care for yourself and thoroughly evaluate the benefits and drawbacks of relationships and business opportunities. With lowest Water, you also may not do a great job of pausing regularly to recover from your busy existence. Additionally, those who score lowest in the Water archetype may find it challenging to find solutions to their own problems, relying upon and asking too many people for their opinions on what to do. Those with lowest Water may believe it's a waste of time to rest and are more likely to feel more confident in relationships than going solo.

Having an awareness of your lowest archetype, however, can show you where you need to focus your efforts for building overall resilience to daily stress. Additionally, recognizing that Water is your lowest force and doing the work to increase Water characteristics propels you to build more rewarding interpersonal relationships and improves your ability to listen without judgment.

THE FIVE ARCHETYPES METHOD

Optimization

The Five Archetypes method begins with optimization, a process that comprises three steps, which remain the same no matter which archetype is your primary. They are:

1. Recognize your primary archetype's strength and stress states.
2. Understand your primary archetype's individual needs for safety.
3. Achieve balance within your primary archetype.

As a result of optimizing your primary archetype, you will cultivate more empathy and compassion—for yourself and others—and replace old, ineffectual patterns with empowerment. You will embody stability and security in the face of upset. Optimization will also give you elegance and agility at times when you're feeling powerless or tossed about like a rudderless sailboat in response to unpredictable and unstable predicaments—and help you navigate those unchartered waters with more grace and stability.

Step One:
Recognizing Water's Strength and Stress States

When your Water is balanced, you will notice that it contributes the strengths of deep knowledge, enlightenment, contentment, and courage to your life, your relationships, and the broader global community.

A balanced Water also helps us:

+ Seek deeper wisdom and knowledge about topics that inspire us.
+ Appreciate the wonder of getting lost in the deliciousness of a terrific book.
+ Remain steadfastly loyal to our friends and family.
+ Avoid being drawn into other people's drama.
+ Remain properly hydrated by drinking enough water.
+ Get good sleep.
+ Refrain from reacting quickly to intense emotions and feelings.
+ Take our time evaluating and creating a thorough plan before executing it.
+ Gain joy from learning and broadening our knowledge base.
+ Feel all right about not knowing what to do right away when there's a conflict.
+ Look back and reflect on the events of a day to view them in a new light, allowing for the manifestation of new problem-solving strategies.
+ Achieve deep meditative states.
+ Pay attention to our own voice of reason.
+ Notice small, important problem-solving clues we wouldn't notice if we weren't emotionally quiet enough inside.

+ Become more consistently self-conscious and self-aware.
+ Practice discernment about our private lives.
+ Understand and write insightful poetry.
+ Appreciate the beauty in the stillness of winter.
+ Avoid divulging important details of classified or private projects and relationships.

We create a peaceful sense of calm and balance in our lives and in the lives of others when we can easily access the positive aspects of our Water archetype. But sometimes our Water becomes unstable, stressed, and unavailable to us. When this happens, we don't feel a sense of certitude, and it's difficult to solve problems for ourselves or in our relationships. Luckily, Water gives us warning signs to help us know when this is happening.

Stressed Water manifests as:

+ Not getting enough sleep.
+ Not drinking enough water.
+ Forgetting to eat or eating too much.
+ Thinking and fantasizing too much.
+ Isolating yourself much more than socializing.
+ Becoming forgetful.
+ Misplacing things like keys, phones, wallets.
+ Feeling depressed.
+ Worrying about the future.
+ Not feeling motivated to work on ideas you usually feel proud of and excited about.
+ Feeling hopeless.
+ Spending so much time thinking about how to solve a problem that you miss the opportunity altogether.
+ Being so introverted that you avoid building loving or promising relationships.

+ Losing track of time.
+ Being so averse to establishing a routine that you don't maintain a supportive self-care regimen.
+ Obsessing about dying or being sick.
+ Acting so eccentric or detached that people around you feel you're unapproachable.
+ Over-avoiding public and social activities.
+ Fear that you'll always be alone.
+ Feeling too easily annoyed by people who try to make specific plans with you.

At its core, recognizing your strong and stressed Water characteristics in Step One is about shifting how you use your time. Many of us rush through life, hoping everything goes well and nothing gets in the way of our ticking off all the items on our to-do list. In such a state, we are more likely to ignore the early signs of internal stress and relationship problems. However, early detection allows us to stave off issues well before they become annoying, difficult situations.

Step One in the optimization process invites you to make time to notice subtle clues that may direct you to course-correct, or perhaps to stay right where you are and move a little faster toward your goal.

Start practicing this step by recognizing and tracking your Water stress and strength states. Recognizing asks you to look and observe, not judge and criticize. There is no right or wrong, good or bad in these states. They're your teachers. They help you know what type of action to take so you continue to develop internal strength and expand healthy relationship skills. Just notice your feelings and thoughts when you decide to engage in and sustain—or, alternately, to avoid—smiling at or making eye contact with someone who's looking at you. Become aware of when you're being overly negative about potential events or projects. Familiarize yourself with these things, and remember to simply pay attention to your Water tendencies.

Once you get used to noticing when and how your Water states make themselves apparent in your daily life, you may also choose to track your symptoms or challenge states. Many people are pleasantly surprised at how easy it becomes to take more control over their more challenging states and to self-regulate just by taking a little time to notice their inclinations throughout the day.

Over time, you may surprise yourself by spotting patterns of thoughts and behaviors you usually miss when moving through your day detached from the motivations behind your actions. When you slow down and make a concerted effort to notice your Water states, you're more likely to become aware that your stress thoughts and behaviors always reach a peak around certain types of people in your life. You may notice that when you can take your time getting things done for a new client because there's no strict deadline, you usually feel more resilient to the times when people want to excessively engage in small talk when you never really realized that connection before. You may also start to become cognizant of the fact that you don't need to spend inordinate amounts of time with close friends and family to demonstrate how much you care about them, which is different from how some others engage in relationships. In those moments, you may begin to appreciate the unique value of your Water gift of silence and retreat in nurturing the growth of relationships. The more you pay close attention to your Water tendencies in your daily interactions, the more frequently and clearly you'll recognize with empathy the impact your Water thoughts, behaviors, and propensities have on other people.

Step Two:
Understanding Water's Needs for Safety

You now know how Water looks and feels when it's strong and when it's stressed, but let's take a look at why primary Waters get stressed out in the first place.

As Dr. Cowan teaches in the Tournesol Kids #PowerUp program—a nonprofit we created together to teach parents, teachers, and kids the skills for self-awareness, self-regulation, and empathy—we only experience our stress states when our particular needs for safety are not met. Our individual needs for feeling secure correspond directly to our primary archetype. Just as Water's strength and stress conditions are unique, so are the particular needs a primary Water type requires to feel balanced and avoid feeling too much stress.

For example, you'll see in the list on the next page that primary Water people require regular quiet time and space to think through ideas and solve problems. When Water people go too long without these needs being met, their stressed behaviors and feelings begin manifesting. However, it's up to them to recognize which of their needs are not being met and to make a plan to bring peace and calm back into their lives. If primary Waters were to expect others to meet their needs for adequate space and quiet, they would be setting themselves up for disappointment, which leads to aggravation and annoyance toward themselves and toward the people who "don't get" them. Ultimately, expecting others to fulfill your needs for you only drives a wedge in your relationships and stokes emotions that make it difficult for you to access your naturally wise Water gifts.

This is why I've created a "needs list" for primary Waters, inspired by what I've learned from Dr. Cowan, so you as a Philosopher can better understand your specific needs and avoid getting stuck in situations that distract you from your gentle path. Recognizing and meeting your individual needs for safety will help you feel articulate, protected, and motivated to take good care of yourself and your relationships.

NOTE: If Water is not your primary archetype, you can still refer to this Water's Needs List to better understand and empathize with the primary Water people in your life. The more skilled you become at empathizing with the needs of others, the more success you'll have in your interpersonal relationships. For more information on how to more harmoniously interact with the other Water types in your life, turn to page 264.

WATER'S NEEDS LIST

- Accuracy
- Alone time
- Assurance
- Autonomy
- Calm
- Commitment
- Concentration
- Contemplation
- Courage
- Creativity
- Deep thought
- Dependability
- Determination
- Dignity
- Discretion
- Downtime
- Fantasy

- Flexibility
- Genuineness
- Honor
- Imagination
- Immersion
- Inference
- Information
- Inquiry
- Insight
- Integrity
- License
- Listening
- Meaning
- Meditation
- Observation
- Patience
- Peace

- Privacy
- Proficiency
- Recess
- Reflection
- Reliability
- Respite
- Rest
- Self-control
- Self-sufficiency
- Significance
- Silence
- Sincerity
- Sleep
- Space
- Toleration
- Tranquility
- Trust

WATER'S NEEDS LIST (CONTINUED)

+ Truth   + Volition
+ Understanding   + Water

If your primary archetype is Water, use the needs list to help you:

+ Feel relief more quickly in times of challenge.
+ Feel less critical of yourself and others.
+ Feel more motivated to figure out how to have your own needs met more of the time.

To help you get started, think of a current struggle you're having. Then take a look over the needs list to see if there is a need related to your struggle that you wish you could fulfill right now.

Be mindful that this needs exercise is not about what others aren't giving you or doing for you, as Dr. Cowan teaches. Instead, it's about gaining an awareness of which of your core needs for safety are not being met at that moment and figuring out what *you* can do to have your needs met.

Keep in mind, your individual "needs" work is about empowering yourself to observe how you're feeling and to take control over creating internal harmony. It's about figuring out how you can get your own needs met, not about expecting other people or outside circumstances to change so that you get what you want. I'd be willing to bet you've tried that before and have come up empty-handed. Expecting others to complete us simply doesn't work—sorry, Jerry McGuire!

This is not to say we shouldn't empathize with and care for each other or meet each other's needs within relationships. The sign of a strong relationship is when we can have compassion for and meet each other's shared needs for safety. Take a look back over Neha Chawla's advice for building and nurturing strong relationships on pages 36–38 for a refresher.

Remember that the only thing in this world you can control is you. Take some time to review the needs list that corresponds to your primary archetype. When your stress states creep up, pause instead of reacting. Then practice taking action to acquire the items on the list that you need in your life. Doing so will reduce the frequency and severity of your stress states and allow you to recover from them more quickly and easily. As a result, you'll feel better more of the time and enjoy more fulfilling relationships.

The highest level of having your needs met is being able to meet them for yourself. Being aware of and figuring out how to meet your needs for safety is the way to continuously grow stronger throughout your lifetime. When you're self-aware, self-reliant, empathetic, and empowered to meet your own needs, your life experience is exponentially elevated.

Step Two in the optimization process requires that you recognize which specific unmet Water needs for safety are initiating your unpleas-ant emotions. The more you practice noticing your stress and strength states, the easier it will be for you to identify and even predict why you're feeling low. Making this connection subsequently brings you closer to taking control over the seemingly inexplicable ebb and flow of your emo-tions.

For example, a frequent stress trigger for primary Water people is feeling inextricably tied to someone else's timeline. When primary Waters feel pressured to conform to a particular schedule, their fear of not having enough time and space to adequately make decisions is roused. In the face of such fear, a primary Water person may become grouchy, aggravated, and absentminded, and seek to escape and be alone.

When left unaddressed, these worrisome emotions magnify. In Water types, this intensification could result in:

+ Expressions of panic, fear, and dread.
+ Worsening sleep problems.
+ Believing there is no way out of this heaviness becoming ever more of a challenge.

To start practicing Step Two as a primary Water, examine a current stressor that's bothering you. Next, identify the feelings that come up for you as a result of this particular challenge. Your emotions are your need identifiers. Water types sometimes react to challenging situations by feeling a sense of alarm or trepidation. However, here I'm asking you to pause with these uncomfortable emotions instead of reacting to them and consider that your feelings are there to help you identify your unmet needs for safety in this moment. Once you've identified your feelings, pause for a moment and ask yourself what unmet need(s) the emotions are telling you that you should focus on from your needs list.

If you're feeling anxious, afraid, indifferent, or withdrawn, Step Two asks you to notice it. Observe and don't react. Try to identify what your frightful Water emotions are telling you that you need in that moment. Are you feeling pressure from other people about a looming deadline? Are your friends or coworkers pushing you to participate in too many non-essential group activities? Are people around you being too dramatic or asking you to make decisions you're not ready to make?

Any of these examples can push buttons for primary Water people, but the more you practice pausing and observing what comes up for you in challenging situations, the more you'll remain calm and notice which of your needs aren't being met instead of experiencing a lack of confidence or self-critical thinking. When you know what is causing your Water energy to get caught up in fright and apprehension, you grow closer to becoming more resilient to your triggers on a regular basis.

Step Three:
Achieving Balance Within the Water Archetype

Step Three in the optimization process is about taking action. This is the step for building your foundation of resilience and making new stress-response choices. This is where you begin to build new habits and behaviors, which translate into the creation of new and healthier neural pathways over time and, ultimately, to balance within your primary archetype.

Armed with new information about the source of your stressors from Step Two, you're more aware of where your unpleasant feelings are coming from. You understand that they're directly related to whether or not you're having your needs for safety met. Other people and outside circumstances may initiate uncomfortable events, but how you choose to respond is ultimately your decision. If you elect to react while your Water is unbalanced, you and those around you will spend more time in discomfort.

On the other hand, if your Water is balanced, you will be more in control of your reactive states under stress and actually reduce the amount of time you and the others spend in uneasiness. Reducing your reactivity enables clear thinking, creative problem solving, smoother conflict resolution, and limitless compassion for yourself and others. When you have more control over your stress reactions, you will live a more fulfilling and well-adjusted life.

Let's get to the core of how to cultivate a balanced Water archetype. While Water is the power of understanding the deeper meanings behind everyday occurrences, if it's not nurtured and channeled properly, it can distort your ability to share your brilliance with the world. The Water archetype needs to support you by contributing its steady and articulate guidance, not its stressed qualities. You also need your Water to be balanced so it can help temper and balance the stress states of the other four archetypes within you. Ultimately, as a primary Water, your Water archetype needs to work for you so it can improve your life, instead of making it stressful.

Your Water-Balancing Skills

Balanced Water presents itself as the ability to consistently access and share our wisdom with the world, while patiently teaching others to access their own determination, courage, and capabilities.

As you know, Water is guided by the need to create an existence steeped in purposeful meaning. Waters are deeply devoted to their family and small circle of friends. But just as water without boundaries disappears deep into the ground or, on the surface, evaporates under too much heat, Water's instability can manifest as becoming too unfocused or as withdrawing completely.

We become balanced by taking specific and consistent action that builds and protects the body, mind, and spirit components of our archetypal nature. Eastern well-being philosophies like TCM state that whole health is not achieved by simply addressing one of these three aspects of our overall being. They teach that these three aspects are inextricably connected within us. For example, a physical imbalance is likely to cause emotional unrest that, left unmanaged, can manifest as larger existential conundrums. Consummate balance is the result of a combined effort to empower all three intertwined parts. You'll notice that the tasks for balancing all five archetypes draw upon all three realms: mind, body, and spirit.

+ + + + +

Now that you're familiar with Steps One and Two of the optimization process, in which you learned about Water's archetypal traits and needs for safety, it's time to learn how to balance your Water archetype—and even how to help other Water types do the same.

There are two important ways of doing so:

+ Self-care in the moment
+ Long-term maintenance

Water Self-Care in the Moment

Water self-care in a moment of emotional alarm requires specific archetypal skills, which are different from those you'll use for building resilience over time. Faced with an exceedingly difficult situation, a primary Water person will have a hard time avoiding growing feelings of aggravation and withdrawal. In these heightened states of stress, primary Waters will also not have easy access to their usually outstanding ability to problem solve.

But in Water's most frustrating moments, such as when fear and negative thinking become exceptionally intense, Wood serves as Water's immediate stress-release valve. Wood activities, behaviors, thoughts, and people are all great at soothing Water types and helping them recover quickly from stress.

Some Wood tools for releasing the initial pressure include:

* Get moving. Take a walk to get your emotions and brilliant ideas moving.
* Practice a hip- and lower-back-opening yoga stretch, or a twist such as a low lunge, cat/cow pose, or supine twist.
* Go outside and be in nature. Literally change your current perspective.
* Plan your next two moves—looking to the future motivates you to propel your creative ideas out of your imagination and apply them in the world.
* Imagine how your concepts and solutions are going to impact people and systemic problems tomorrow, next week, and for generations to come.
* List two things you want to accomplish this week, and come up with a due date for each.
* Name three choices you have for taking control of this situation.

+ Remind yourself how far you've come toward reaching your goal.

Once the severity of the emotions subsides and a calm sensibility returns, primary Waters regain the composure to mobilize skills from all five archetypes to help resolve the problem that initiated the feelings of insecurity in the first place.

When you, as a primary Water, feel adequately composed and prepared to begin problem solving, choose the archetype-based activities from the lists on pages 258–63 that correspond to the strengths you most need in the moment. Examples of the strengths that correspond to each type are:

+ **Wood:** You'll need to rely upon your Wood skills if your problem requires a plan, forward movement, or speed.
+ **Fire:** You'll need to draw upon your Fire skills if your problem requires optimism, deepening connections with people, or discussing your feelings.
+ **Earth:** You'll need to access your Earth skills if your issue requires collaboration with another party, teaching others a skill, or gaining an understanding of what everyone needs next.
+ **Metal:** You'll want to dip into your Metal skills if your concern revolves around creating a timeline, developing a new system, holding yourself or someone else accountable, or correcting and editing a document.
+ **Water:** You'll reach for your Water skills if your issue requires more time to think things through, a deeper evaluation of all the components impacting your challenge, or sitting back and really listening to everyone else's ideas and concerns.

Water Long-Term Maintenance

Another way to achieve balance in your Water archetype is to practice your maintenance activities over the long term to ensure you remain resilient in the face of stress as you progress. With a strong, reliable foundation of resilience built over time, you will be better able to observe your challenges and not react to them. The better you become at avoiding reactive states, the more quickly you recover from stress and return to enjoying life.

Begin your maintenance regimen by practicing activities that support your primary Water archetype. Start first by choosing one or two activities from the Water list to practice every day.

Next, identify one or two activities from the archetype list that correspond to the archetype in which you scored the lowest. Add these items to your daily Water archetype routine. Don't forget, it's important to practice your lowest archetype, even if it's your least favorite type of activity (which I'm willing to bet it is). Exercising your most vulnerable archetype minimizes the gap between your highest and lowest archetypes, expanding your ability to be more emotionally dexterous when challenges arise.

Finally, practice activities that correlate to the challenges you're currently facing. Here are some examples to help you identify which archetypal skills in the lists on pages 50–59 you will need and will find most helpful as a primary Water:

- If you're stuck in a constant loop of imaginatively thinking about how a new invention or strategy may manifest, add in some Wood-building activities to help you bring your ideas to fruition more quickly.
- If you find yourself being overly wary, negative, or skeptical about engaging in new relationships and projects, practice some Fire activities.
- If you're avoiding collaborating with others on a project, even if you know their input could be helpful,

empower your ability to work as part of a team with some Earth-building activities.

+ If you're having a hard time being punctual or remembering to eat meals on a regular schedule, it's time to exercise your Metal skills.

Choose from among these Water activities to get you started on building your Water maintenance regimen:

+ Recognize and track the times when you have little patience for people with boisterous personalities or when you avoid people who always want you to participate in group activities. In those moments, see if you can reframe your thinking and recognize the benefit their gregariousness contributes.

+ Give yourself regular free time—a gentle, quiet time and space for yourself each day to be alone. Spend the time however you feel is most refreshing for your wellbeing. Read a book, take a slow walk, think about a fantasy, write a poem, bird-watch, take a leisurely swim.

+ Make sure you're drinking enough water each day.

+ Get good sleep each night.

+ Find and practice activities that hold meaning for you at work and in your hobbies.

+ Develop a meditation practice that is relevant and meaningful to you.

+ Observe and track times when you choose not to share your ideas with others.

+ Pay attention to the times you feel compelled to withdraw from communication or relationships. Just observe; don't judge yourself for it.

- Recognize when you're feeling fearful of being vulnerable or making the wrong decision.
- Recognize when you're spending too much time thinking or daydreaming.
- Track your specific stress triggers and patterns so you can have more control over them in the future.
- Listen to soothing music.
- Imagine how you'll feel when stressful situations are resolved.
- Experiment with metaphor. Define what current or past dilemmas remind you of, or what they feel like.

Metal-Building Activities

- Schedule your day so you don't spend too much time getting lost in your thoughts or imagination.
- Establish an area of your home for storing things you need each day, and use it. Put your keys, phone, wallet, sunglasses, anything small that can easily get misplaced around the house in that area.
- Create some structured time for a spiritual practice of your choice.
- Keep a calendar of your activities and follow it.
- Come up with a strategy for measuring your success in keeping up with your routines and remaining on time with projects and appointments.
- Adopt a breathwork practice that you like, and do it regularly.
- Upon waking and right before you fall asleep at night, think of people for whom you're grateful.
- Participate in self-care that gives you personalized attention, like acupuncture or Ayurveda.

+ The sense of smell correlates to the Metal archetype. Use aromatherapy at home and at work, if appropriate. Aromas that support balanced Water include:

+ Black pepper	+ Vetiver	+ Frankincense
+ Rosemary	+ Angelica	+ Lavender
+ Cedar wood	+ Ginger	

+ Choose or create your own ritual that means something to you and practice it regularly. See if you can practice at or around the same time each day.
+ Create a special space in your home and dedicate it to a quiet activity, which could be reading, meditating, praying, or journaling.
+ Practice something that requires coordination and focus to get better, like playing a musical instrument or creating a painting or sculpture.
+ Observe negative thoughts that arise about yourself, others, and situations. Notice them, and then see if you can practice letting them go with a firm exhale through the mouth.
+ Practice creating small, easily accomplished routines for yourself. This could include a morning routine, bedtime routine, mealtime routine, exercise routine, or simply a specific time during the day when you devote time to connecting with loved ones.

Wood-Building Activities

+ Take some time each day to think about what you need, and make a plan for how you're going to have your needs met. This can be anything from making sure you eat three meals a day to asking for help shopping for groceries.

+ Create a regular exercise routine. Consider incorporating practices that combine breathing with stretching and moving, like yoga, qi gong, or tai chi.

+ Come up with a list of goals each month, and stay on target to achieve them. If this is tough for you, start small, with goals that are easy to reach, and over time increase the complexity of the goals you set for yourself.

+ Surround yourself with colors that soothe you. Consider red, orange, and earthy tones.

+ Go outside and spend time in nature.

+ Once per week, imagine the next two steps you need to take to implement one of your ideas so other people can learn and benefit from it. Create and follow through with a plan for at least one of the two steps.

+ Consider trying manual therapies like massage or craniosacral therapy.

Fire-Building Activities

+ Build in time during the week to relax with friends and enjoy fun activities together.

+ Practice articulating your feelings, even if you just start by expressing them to yourself. Recognize how you feel at different moments during the day. Over time, you will become more aware of your fluctuating emotions and will develop more empathy for other people's changing emotions as well.

+ Smile at yourself in the mirror at some point each day. It's said that smiling reduces cortisol production.

- Practice heart-opening yoga stretches like the bow pose, camel pose, cobra pose, cow pose, and fish pose.
- When you feel a skeptical thought arise regarding a new colleague or potential project, pause and imagine what a more trusting perspective of the same encounter might look like for you. You don't have to follow this more un-suspecting viewpoint. This mind-set exercise expands your ability to empathize with Fire ways of thinking.
- Make a list of what aspects of your life you believe are private, and write down why you feel those things are private. Imagine what it would be like to share one of the least private items from your list with a close friend. You may even consider actually sharing this information with another person.

Earth-Building Activities

- Find a community you appreciate being part of and devote some time to participating in their activities.
- Consider volunteering for a nonprofit whose mission aligns with your sense of personal meaning.
- Once per day, practice identifying what someone in your family or at work needs and provide it to them. It could be advice, a compassionate ear, help with er-rands, cleaning up the kitchen after a meal, or extra time finishing a project.
- Make sure you're eating well and that you have healthy digestion. Pay attention to eating meals at a regular time. Notice whether you feel constipated, gassy, or bloated, or if you have acid reflux. If your digestion feels shaky, seek the guidance of a nutrition specialist to get it back on track.

- Find one item or meal to eat mindfully each day, appreciating every bite, chewing slowly, and pausing between bites. Consider trying to chew twenty times per bite.
- Close your eyes and bring your awareness to your body. Can you identify where your current stress sits in your body right now? Observe it, breathe into that spot, and exhale with strength through your mouth, imagining that the exhale is releasing the stress through the spot on your body where you envisioned it having been lodged.
- Practice engaging in sociable exchanges every once in a while for the sole purpose of showing you care about another person. Ask questions about their day, their family, or their work, and share something about yourself to expand your comfort level with having a casual, caring, personal conversation. Take note of what thoughts, feelings, and body manifestations come up for you during these chats.

Ultimately, your Water archetype is balanced when you:

- Have more control over your feelings of discomfort in the face of change and other people's deadlines.
- Notice more quickly when you begin getting lost in your thoughts, fantasies, or imagination.
- Get good sleep.
- Don't shy away from creating consistent self-care routines, like eating at regular intervals, setting a regular bedtime, or meditating at the same time each day.
- Feel more comfortable trusting your gut or intuition when making quick decisions.

+ Begin to feel more relaxed in social situations and in building friendly relationships with people.
+ Are more open to appreciating what you may learn from participating in brainstorming meetings.
+ Don't lose your keys as much.
+ Become more tolerant of participating in casual conversations.
+ Spend less time isolating when you feel insecure.
+ Are less hyperaware of your internal thoughts during conversations and in group settings.
+ Have an easier time implementing and carrying out your ideas.
+ Enjoy a little structure in your day.
+ Are more consciously aware of your strength and stress states.
+ Experience more balanced moods.
+ Are able to predict triggers and know your needs for safety.
+ Are able to have your needs met, and self-regulate with ease in times of stress.
+ Experience less fear about the future and about the possibility of making the wrong choice.
+ Are less filled with dread at the possibility of being defenseless or exposed in front of others.

Harmonization

I don't want to leave you hanging, wondering when and how you'll know you're in harmony as a primary Water.

Again, harmonization is not an absence of stress and challenge. For primary Waters, it's about being able to navigate the challenging moments of your own life while empathizing with and supporting those around you whose Water archetype may be low and in need of a boost. At its core, harmonization allows you to have unconditional love for yourself and those around you.

When you, as a primary Water, are harmonized, you're likely to experience many, if not all, of the attitudes and behaviors noted below.

- You consistently notice, honor, and take control over the connections
  - between the quantity and quality of rest you get and how often you react in fear or dread when you feel triggered.
  - between how much you routinize your day and how often you become lost in your imagination.
  - between how often you make plans and take specific action to realize your ideas and the amount of time you spend enjoying a sense of internal peace.
  - between devoting time to creating and maintaining relationships and how deeply you withdraw in the face of stress.
  - between how mindful you are of your shifting emotions and how comfortable you feel attending social gatherings.
- People seek you out more for advice and guidance.
- You're better able to balance and enjoy your alone time as well as more intimate and even bigger social activities.
- Your eating habits are more structured by eating full meals rather than grazing throughout the day.
- Your wake and sleep patterns are more aligned to the circadian rhythm of the rise and fall of melatonin and cortisol.
- You become more curious about other people and situations outside your vivid imagination.

+ You have more excitement for life and what gifts it may bring each day.

+ You enjoy the give-and-take of conversation and are more curious about what you can learn from the people around you.

+ You catch yourself more quickly if you begin to feel dispassionate about your life, your ideas, your relationships, and your possibilities for future growth.

+ You have more interest in forming bonds with new people in your life.

+ You open up and listen to others' opinions and needs when you would normally be a stubborn supporter of your own view.

+ You can hold steady and not follow your inclination to retreat when the circumstances in your environment shift unexpectedly.

+ You are led more by introspection and objectivity than by suspicion and pessimism.

WATER IN RELATIONSHIPS

As our personal awareness and resilience in the face of stress expands, we are less triggered by other people's opinions, moods, and tendencies. We also become less likely to attach to relationships that don't serve us well or in which our needs for safety aren't being met. As we strengthen our individual Five Archetypes skills, we are better equipped to form equally strong bonds with individuals from any one of the Five Archetypes because we see the benefit and the beauty of the gifts they each bring to the companionship.

In this section, Waters will gain guidance for building and maintaining propitious relationships, and non-primary Waters will learn how to engage in healthy relationships with primary Water types.

If You Are a Water/Philosopher

To be a good Water partner in any relationship, practice staying in balance by knowing your strengths, challenges, and needs, and by practicing the Water long-term maintenance activities beginning on page 258 to remain a consistently stable partner. This will ensure that you approach relationship challenges from a place of calm compassion for yourself and your companions.

When you commit to doing the work that keeps your Water in balance, you contribute the following strengths to your interpersonal relationships:

- Remaining calm in the face of high-stress, high-panic situations.
- Devoting yourself to your closest friends and family.
- Not getting too caught up in other people's drama.
- Spending one-on-one time together with your loved one instead of going out and socializing too much.
- Listening deeply to what your partner needs.
- Solving complicated problems with ease, such as whose family to be with for holidays.
- Not needing to rely on your partner to take care of all your needs and emotions, but instead being self-reliant.
- Imagining a creative, simple way out of an entangled argument.
- Drilling down to the root of communication problems, and recommending a path to healing them.
- Articulating precisely and poetically what you love about your partner.
- Creating and perpetuating deep meaning in relationships.

+ Having a willingness to put in the effort to grow together within the relationship.
+ Giving your partner alone time.
+ Maintaining an honest interest in getting to know
  your partner.
+ Being naturally introspective, less likely to blame your
  partner for your own emotions and feelings.

When your primary Water is balanced, you also possess the following characteristics that benefit the global community:

+ You seek to solve big problems in new ways and to
  figure out what's needed to effect the new solution.
+ You draw from a vast, wise knowledge base and memory when designing the way forward.
+ You listen to all aspects of a situation and gather the
  pertinent information before making a decision about
  how to move forward to ensure the best plan is created.
+ You inject a sense of peaceful reason and help calm
  other team members when emotions become heated
  so that everyone stays the course and remains focused
  on the goal at hand.
+ You teach others the importance of quiet reflection
  and taking time to let ideas simmer so that everyone
  has better access to their own ability to contribute
  creatively to the greater cause.
+ You create innovative and broad, sweeping plans that
  span divergent missions, cultures, and communities
  to make the world a better place.

On the other hand, when your primary Water is not in balance, it
shows up in your interpersonal relationships as:

+ Wanting to be alone when things get tough.
+ Not talking enough about what you're feeling.
+ Preferring to spend time by yourself rather than with others.
+ Becoming too suspicious of your partner's intentions.
+ Losing hope in the relationship without talking things through.
+ Not feeling safe enough to be completely vulnerable with your partner.
+ Never wanting to go to parties or family holiday gatherings.
+ Believing the worst about the future of the relationship.
+ Forgetting important milestones and dates.
+ Becoming too stubborn, thinking your way is the only way.
+ Completely shutting down to the possibility of working things out.

When your primary Water is unbalanced, watch out for these potential behaviors that could manifest and affect your global community:

+ Spending too much time trying to figure out how to fix big problems without implementing any of the plans.
+ Not seeing the benefit in collaborating with a team because you know all the answers already.
+ Having trouble structuring your time effectively and getting lost merely thinking of good ideas.
+ Becoming too removed from how others feel.
+ Becoming overly quiet or over-isolated.
+ Not easily sharing your insightful ideas with others, so people can't benefit from your ingenuity.

+ Feeling so fearful you'll make the wrong decision about what to do and how to solve problems that you end up doing nothing.
+ Becoming so negative about your own abilities that you stop engaging with the community or team.
+ Overthinking how to fix systemic problems.
+ Losing the desire to make the world a better place and to fight for what you know is right.

If You Have a Relationship with a Water/Philosopher

In the following pages, you will learn how primary Waters exhibit themselves at work, in intimate relationships, and as parents. Remember, *The Five Archetypes* is a primer for beginners, so I'm just touching on the basic concepts to help you understand, evaluate, and adjust the flow of the primary Water archetype within you for the best personal and interpersonal outcomes.

The Water Employee or Coworker

When applied to the workplace, the Five Archetypes method expands your ability and the ability of your coworkers to get things done efficiently. Moreover, when employees and colleagues feel safe, seen, understood, and appreciated in the workplace, they navigate challenges more easily and therefore are less reactive when in stress states, which ultimately translates to a healthier bottom line.

To enhance your awareness of times when your Water staff or coworkers feel safe and when they feel insecure, there are some common tendencies to watch out for. When you see your colleagues exhibiting their insecure states, it's time to pause and fortify yourself so you don't jump into your reactive states as a result. Get to know these common strengths, needs, and stress states:

+ Strengths at Work: Water staff are self-sufficient, insightful, knowledge-seeking, and introspective. They're imaginative and have a great memory for people and experiences. Waters are great listeners, and they understand how to solve complex problems.

+ Needs at Work: Waters require quiet, space, and time to process thoughts and information in order to access their strengths in solving complex issues.

+ Potential Challenges and Stress States: When Water people feel insecure and their needs for safety aren't met, they become fearful and withdraw or disengage. Under stress, Water can think too much about an idea and never bring it to fruition.

+ Here's how to nurture Water employees over time and how to help them release stress in the moment.

  + Support in the Moment: Redirect your stressed Water employee or coworker by encouraging them to do some form of physical movement, like taking a walk or doing a stretch sequence. If movement isn't an option in the moment, ask your stressed Water employee to envision and plan the next step in the process they feel stuck on. The forward thinking and physical movement can both provide outlets for primary Water's creative ideas that sometimes feel overwhelming, especially if they believe there is no avenue for implementing them at work.

  + Ongoing Encouragement: Nurture a sense of inner peace and consistency for your Water staff by creating routines like regular staff meetings, consistent and clear feedback, and structures and systems within which they will work. The orderliness enhances Water's ability to access their deep insights

271

that help the larger group over time. The reliable routines also provide a sense of safety in the face of social challenges where Water types are more likely to feel isolated within the group.

The Water Friend

Enjoying mutually gratifying friendships starts with *you* knowing how to be a good friend to others. To consistently show up as a steady, sincere, reliable friend, check out these Five Archetypes guidelines:

+ Learn your primary archetype strengths, challenges, and needs so you can practice becoming and staying self-aware.
+ Make sure your needs for safety are being met within the relationship.
+ Recognize and take responsibility for your reactive states and practice your self-regulation techniques.
+ Adopt a mind-set in which you recognize challenge as an invitation to grow, not an excuse to judge or criticize others.
+ Discover your friends' needs for safety so you can practice compassionate consideration.

How Do We Nurture Lasting Friendships?

As a friendship grows, how do we continue to nurture and strengthen that bond using the Five Archetypes method? When you know your friend's primary archetype, you will better understand what makes them feel safe and what makes them feel insecure. Here are some additional suggestions for what primary Water people will likely appreciate in a close friendship.

Waters like spending time with people who:

+ Prefer staying in to going out and partying too much.
+ Enjoy dissecting the deeper meanings of the movies you see together.
+ Like having a quiet, unplanned, chill afternoon that's not overscheduled.
+ Solve problems rather than talk too much about them.

Helping a Water Friend in Stress

When you care about someone, you sympathize with their pain and want them to feel better. The Five Archetypes model helps us understand that people have unique stress triggers and also have different paths to de-stressing. Here's how to help your primary Water friends recover more quickly from stress states.

Cheer up a Water friend by demonstrating confidence in his abilities. Point out how his wisdom and determination helped you believe in new potential and feel more confident taking courageous action to improve your own life. Water will also benefit from spending time with you doing something methodical, like organizing a closet or rearranging the furniture in a room.

The Water Romantic Partner

Primary Water people bestow a sense of calm groundedness upon a union. Your Water partner will listen to you with patience and stillness to help you gain a broader perspective on your dilemmas. Water will write you a love poem that touches your heart with profound meaning. He makes sure you balance your social life with adequate rest and is fully committed to his family unit. Water will hold you for a long time at night and laze around in bed on Sunday morning for hours like there's no place else in the world to be.

When Water types feel insecure, they exhibit specific patterns of disharmony in a relationship. Stressed Waters fear being vulnerable and making the wrong choice. When they really feel low, they worry about being misunderstood and spend too much time alone, disconnecting from conversation and becoming prone to bouts of depression.

Here are some tips for how you can be a strong partner to a primary Water type.

- ✦ Do: Give him time and space when he asks for it. Water's need for a pause is not a reflection of how much he cares about you but rather the way he most comfortably works through his stressed feelings.
- ✦ Don't: Flit around at a party paying attention to everyone in the room but him. He likes to know he's important to you. Don't require that he attend every family or friend gathering. Give him a break. He needs his quiet time to be at his best.
- ✦ Help Him Refocus in Stress: Get stressed Water outside and moving. While you're out, tell him how much you admire his wisdom and that you're confident in his ability to get through challenging times. Sometimes you don't have to talk at all. Just be there next to him.
- ✦ Best Form of Consistent Encouragement: Include your Water partner in household projects like redecorating or restoring antiques. The creative endeavor will keep him from spending too much time alone and give you some great projects to complete together, strengthening your bond.

The Parent–Water Child Relationship

Your parent-child relationship is impacted not only by the intersection between your and your child's primary archetypes but also by how you perceive your purpose as a parent. When you see your parental role as compassionate guide and teacher and empower your kids to master life skills so they become strong, resilient adults, you're more likely to build a strong relationship with your child and feel fulfilled by the parenting journey.

To create a gratifying and lasting relationship with your primary Water child using the Five Archetypes method, start by identifying and balancing your own primary archetype. Get to know yourself in strength and in stress. Understand your button pushers so that you're best able to remain in a state of resilience and compassionate power when faced with your triggers. You'll be the most outstanding advocate and nurture a respectful, strong relationship with your child when you serve as a heroic example of how to manage stress, triggers, and disappointment.

Then find out your child's primary archetype. Help him become more self-aware and self-reliant by teaching him how to recognize and celebrate his gifts. Empower him to overcome stress states with ease by understanding what pushes his buttons and giving him the Five Archetypes tools to become more resilient to his triggers.

As you know, Dr. Cowan is a pioneer of using the five types as a methodology for healthy child development. Here are some points, inspired by his work, to keep in mind when parenting a child whose primary archetype is Water:

+ Learning style: Water kids learn by imagination, reflection, and metaphor. They appreciate taking their time with material and don't like to be rushed as they learn new skills and information.

+ Sleeping: Water kids may get caught up in reading or lost in their imagination late into the night. Nurture healthy sleep habits by creating a bedtime routine that over time reminds the body and mind that it's time for bed. Such a routine could include a soothing bath, lowering the lights, peaceful music, a hand and foot massage with coconut oil, putting Brahmi oil on the forehead, chanting *Om* a few times to naturally stimulate melatonin production, and/or a short breathing exercise.

+ Eating: Water kids tend to have less patience for paying attention to the needs of the body. Create meaning around food, mealtime, and grocery shopping so they can achieve higher levels of enjoyment when it comes to nutrition.

+ Exercise: Water kids are less drawn to group exercise classes. Introduce them to movement programs they can excel at individually and in which they personally find meaning.

+ Feelings: When Water kids are not at their best, they tend to become fearful and wonder if they will become irrelevant. Make sure your Water kids understand that feelings are constantly in flux, so they develop more patience and empathy for themselves and others and remain engaged instead of retreating into sad or depressive states.

WATER AYURVEDIC PRACTICES

Water people prefer wellness activities that don't require conformity to someone else's specific or strict timeline. They'll gravitate toward individual pursuits they find meaningful, rather than joining a group class or a high-energy competitive sport. For example, Water people appreciate the benefits and practice of meditation, but would more likely meditate on their own rather than join an organized class they had to attend at a specific time each day.

Water people may also struggle sticking to a food plan or regimen. They may find it hard to eat enough or to stop mindlessly grazing throughout the day. While they'll thrive with structure, Water people shy away from it, so a diet that offers some amount of flexibility and self-management may work better for them.

If you're a primary Water, focus your wellness pursuits around gentle structure, autonomy, and deep meaning and you will be more likely to stick with the program.

With regard to incorporating Ayurvedic wellness practices into your everyday life, remember that the Water archetype corresponds to the first Chakra. In the chart on the next page, you will find some gentle Ayurvedic practices that will help engage and balance this chakra.

The first Chakra is known as the Root Chakra. According to Ayurveda, the Root Chakra governs security and survival; when in balance, it correlates to Water's courage and steadfast will.

Using Ayurvedic practices is a safe and empowering option to complement any health-care regimen. Peruse the selection of Ayurvedic lifestyle practices below that correspond to your primary Water archetype. Feel free to try the ones that feel like a good fit as you assemble your menu of healthy lifestyle practices.

First Chakra—Root

Oversees: Connection of divine consciousness with material life, connection with Mother Earth, security, survival, physical energy, self-preservation

Location: Base of the spine, kidney, spinal column, back, feet, hips, legs

Color: Red

Mantra: Lam

Yoga: Mountain pose, sun salutations, wide-legged forward fold, bridge pose, savasana

Gemstones: Red garnet, black tourmaline, tiger's eye

Mudra (a hand gesture that's said to stimulate a specific sense of focus and balance): Prithvi mudra, hakini mudra

Foot marma (a pressure point that's said to enhance mind-body balance when massaged): Point on the outside edge of the foot about two inches from the heel at the bottom quarter of the foot

Aromatherapy: Black pepper, rosemary, cedar wood, vetiver, angelica, ginger, frankincense, lavender

Taste: Astringent

A Final Note to Primary Waters

Dear Water Friends,

I want to leave you with some parting thoughts as you ponder your future with a Five Archetypes perspective on life:

Remember, you have an unparalleled capacity to create new methods for solving age-old conundrums. Please remember to share your wisdom, because at times you can get caught up thinking about myriad possibilities rather than enlightening us with your wonderful insights. We are quite moved and appreciative of hearing what you have to offer.

You are singular in your ability to listen, learn new things, and problem solve. I am personally indebted to you for:

* *Compassionately showing me the reflection of myself in your reactions to my Fiery behavior so I more adeptly self-correct.*
* *Teaching me to be less gullible.*
* *Reminding me that there is benefit in meditation even when my Fire would rather be doing absolutely anything else more entertaining.*

I wrote a haiku for you in honor of the gifts you bestow upon the world.

> *Your will runs so deep*
> *A courage that doesn't halt*
> *The world needs you more*

With a humble spirit,
Carey

CONCLUSION

"The world needs you more." The final words of the manuscript danced off my fingertips and landed on the laptop keys, shoring up the last line of the Water archetype haiku. A sweet, satisfied smile emerged behind my eyes, resonating from that mysterious point deep within my heart where dreams intersect with reality. I sat back in my chair to savor the moment, clicked save one final time, and signed off with a humble spirit.

I closed my laptop and, with an audible exhalation, pushed back from my dining room table. I was content. I felt hope for the healing I believed would happen as a result of this book being launched out into the world. As had become my routine over my months of writing, I then made my way over to the green high-back chair in the living room and settled in for twenty minutes of meditation. When I closed my eyes, I conjured a bright image of a life lived in concert with the wisdom of the Five Archetypes. The image took the form of a young child, probably nine or ten years old. The child stood bright-eyed and tall and exuded a pure openness to exploring and transforming all the world's struggles into fodder for personal and communal growing and evolving.

There was a broad square window, and the child pushed it open wide with a heave and then stood there. Beyond the window was a field, vast and blanketed with vibrant green grasses and royal purple lavender. The earth warmly welcomed the child's gaze with the promise of bountiful sustenance for the adventure ahead. The child stood relishing the magic of the stillness and taking in the vision of the ripe land.

The earth beckoned. The child stepped through the window and out into the field. With each footstep, the child received nourishment from the natural surroundings, integrated the sustenance, and shared it back through sparkles that leapt around smiling eyes and a thankful soul. Up ahead, the land met the sky at a horizon bursting with purples, pinks, oranges, and reds. The sun was setting on another day. The child was hopeful and strong and expectant for the surprises and delights that awaited tomorrow and all tomorrows to come.

I realized that, in a way, this image was saying, "Never stop exploring." The magical unfolding of the multilayered texture of your life provides endless opportunities to observe, learn, and expand because the context of each and every ripening moment will serve as your perpetual classroom if you allow it to.

The rubric of the Five Archetypes is your abacus. Plug in the data of your nature, your environment, and your dreams in anticipation of the wonderment the world is about to reveal. Then go ahead and grow, my friend. My primary Fire is elated by what you're about to discover.

With deep, delicious, dancing love,
Carey

ACKNOWLEDGMENTS

I am indebted to Harriet Beinfield, LAc, and Efrem Korngold, LAc, OMD, who penned *Between Heaven and Earth: A Guide to Chinese Medicine* (1991). Their book is the eminent resource on how to understand the practice of Chinese medicine. Their work includes an exquisite original exposition of the Five Phase model and how it has the absolute potential to lead to self-mastery. Harriet and Efrem brought to life the wonder and transformative qualities of the Five Phases, and I am ever grateful. I'm blessed to know them both through Dr. Cowan and to have Harriet serve as board president for Tournesol Kids.

I am also indebted to the following:

Dr. Stephen Cowan for your guidance, wisdom, empathy, inspiration, and grace. Your gift of the Five Phases has forever elevated the way I engage with my internal and external environment.

Dondeena Bradley, Water Woman extraordinaire. I thank the wide, magical, and wonderful universe that I sat at your end of the table at that breakfast.

Theresa DiMasi, who pushes me to higher heights with her Wood energy and reminds me she's always there for me with her Earth empathy. You are a dream of a publisher, and I'm beyond thankful.

Lauren Hummel, my editor—I mean, my "book doula." Your Fire bestowed me with accolades and gold stars in every email, phone call, and meeting. Your Metal helped structure my words and cogent ideas with precision and beauty. Deep bows of appreciation to you.

Sam Ford, director of cultural intelligence; Anja Schmidt, executive editor; Patrick Sullivan, art director; and the rest of the Tiller Press team at Simon & Schuster, thank you, thank you, thank you!

Jane von Mehren and the team at Aevitas, and to Monika Tashman, for having my back.

Peter Casperson, my deeply wise and courageous Water, whose calm, deft insight helps me see the best path forward and keeps my Fire from burning too bright for my own good.

Michael Rosen. My dad. My cheerleader. My protector. My most favorite superhero.

Pat and Irv Zeitlin, my parents, whose love, support, and belief in me propel me to keep facing the sun.

My biggest teachers: my children. My Earth babies, Hannah and Maddie. You ladies are both growing into such magnificent beings. I am ever inspired by your empathy for others and your courage to grow through your challenges. My son, Zach, who still refuses to take the Five Archetypes assessment . . . I'm quite sure you're Metal with a healthy dose of Wood. Your drive to build, create, perfect, and improve what exists amazes me. And that you do it all with compassion and love is extraordinarily heartwarming. I adore every second I spend with you.

Danielle Arroyo, Patricia Belfanti, Belinda Levychin, and Karan Neilson for your good vibes.

The countless people whose paths I cross each day. Thank you. The intersection between you and me is where I begin to put the Five Phases into context and realize their magic.